How to Become a Failure

An Immigrant, A Parent and

His Road to Success

SOULY FARAG

Copyright © 2014 by Souly Farag.
All rights reserved.

ISBN: 1493707132
ISBN 13: 978-1493707133
All scripture is taken from the Holy Bible, New International Version®, niv® Copyright © 1973, 1978, 1984, 2011 by Biblica, Inc.®
Used by permission. All rights reserved worldwide.

This book is dedicated to Kylene, my first grandchild.

Kylene,
　By God's grace, you rescued me from a near-death experience and gave me the desire and willpower to survive. You were only nine months old when you and your mother flew from Indiana to Washington state in response to my open-heart surgery. Seeing your face during my hospital recovery was an inspiration to me as I fought to survive.
　You will always be my guardian angel. I promise you that I will stay healthy until I meet the lucky guy. My goal is to take care of myself until that big day.
　I extend my gratitude to you for your efforts in helping with editing, typing, and organizing this memoir over the course of its writing, all at the tender age of thirteen. I am so proud of you. You are one sharp cookie! Giddu[1] loves you.

1　Arabic word for Grandpa.

Contents

Acknowledgments	vii
Foreword	ix
Chapter One: A Title For This Book	1
Chapter Two: Arrival Of An Immigrant	5
Chapter Three: My Career	11
Chapter Four: My Finances	24
Chapter Five: A Chat With My Daughter	35
Chapter Six: An Outing With The Boys	42
Chapter Seven: Business Luncheon With A Partner	66
Chapter Eight: Dinner With My Family	75
Chapter Nine: Am I Ready to Depart?	88
Chapter Ten: Meet My Family	94
Chapter Eleven: My Final Thoughts to My Kids	111
To Those Considering Immigration	115
Benediction	121
Epilogue	125

Acknowledgments

I have sincere appreciation for my loving parents, who planted the seeds of willpower, perseverance, and determination in me and showed me the road to success.

I give thanks to my lovely wife, Vivian, who has given me abundant support and cooperation. Her helping hands have guided me toward the success I have found.

My four wonderful kids have moved me to be a better man and given me reason to excel in what I do. They are each determined to carry on their heritage of excellence and finish what I could not accomplish in my lifetime.

I also thank my first granddaughter, Kylene, who inspired me to write this book and allowed me to share my life with you through it.

My sincere appreciation goes to the CreateSpace publishing team for their invested hours in making this memoir available worldwide.

Without the persistence of my daughter, Sonia, this book would not have been published. My sincere gratitude is rendered to her for the substantial help she provided in fulfilling my dream. She spent many hours typing, editing, and interfacing with the publishing company.

My gratitude goes out to you for taking the time to read my story, even though I am not rich or famous. I am not a celebrity. I am an ordinary citizen who believed in himself and was inspired by those who refused to fail.

I am grateful to the US government and the Founding Fathers who granted me a visa as an immigrant.

This book is also dedicated to all the immigrants who have come to the United States to prove they could make a better life here for themselves, and to all the parents who are motivated by their ancestors and determined to equip their children to excel in life.

This book was further inspired by a workforce that is determined to accept the challenge of putting energy into seeking and maintaining employment, rather than taking the easy road of handouts.

Foreword

Stories of the immigrant experience in the United States are plentiful. They involve people who are predominantly European and have, over the past six decades, established homes in North America. Many of these stories involve the common themes of family, love, loss, loneliness, and incredible struggle leading to transformational success. This story is rather unique but just as rich, as it involves an Egyptian family who immigrated to the Pacific Northwest seeking employment, a better and safer life, and religious freedom. Along the way, they touched my own family in many moving, memorable, and beautiful ways.

I met the Farag family in 1993, in Moses Lake, Washington. I was a young engineer visiting the Celite Quincy plant for the first time, and Souly insisted that I join his family for dinner. Souly was the quality control engineer for the operation, and since we shared similar backgrounds and values, we quickly became good friends. I remember his four children, sitting directly across from me, smiling and engaging me in conversation and laughter. I remember the incredible warmth, instant friendship, and outreach that their mom extended to me that evening. It was the beginning of a close friendship between our families, and one that has grown stronger and more intimate over the last twenty-one years.

In 1997, I was posted as the plant manager for the same operation and, during the two years prior to Souly's retirement, I worked directly with him to introduce a suite of new products that dramatically improved profitability. My family lived in East Wenatchee, Washington, and we spent plenty of time with Souly, Vivian, and the kids. We also met Souly's brother, Nabil, along with his family, and developed a warm friendship with them.

By this time, my own young family had grown from two to four, and between the kids and the demanding pressures of running the operations, we went through some difficult and testing times. As my wife and I had little to no family support of our own, the Farag family stepped in with love, concern, plenty of jokes at my expense, and friendship. Fond memories of my daughter Sofia's baptism and emotional memories of the birth of my son, Dimitri, include Souly and Vivian. When I reflect on that period of my life, I realize that Souly was instrumental in my development as a young father, husband, and professional.

I left Eastern Washington in 2000, but our families have stayed close over the years through Thanksgiving and Christmas visits. Souly and Vivian's children, Sonia, Sharif, Ramez, and Tony, have all attended college and lead their own beautiful lives today. Over that period, I drew closer to Sharif and Tony and, today, I see them very much as my own younger brothers, enjoying their company and friendship and sharing the professional challenges that each of us face. I also witnessed Souly and Vivian evolving into loving grandparents while maintaining the same bonds of love with their children directly.

When I reflect on what I have learned in my relationship with the Farag family, I come to the idea of what is called "unilateral love." It is the fabric that bonds the family together, promoted by Souly, but put in place and instilled in the children by Vivian. She remains one of the most loving and extraordinary people I have ever met.

Unilateral love is simply love with no strings attached. It involves spending quality, meaningful time with each other and giving more than you take. Years ago, I realized that the Farag family calls this *visiting*. They visit with each other, with family, with children, and with friends in a unique and direct way, giving each other 100 percent of their attention, compassion, and sincerity. Advice is given and received, bonds are reestablished, and friendships are strengthened.

There is no right time or wrong time to visit. During Thanksgiving two years ago, my wife and I were helping in Vivian's kitchen. Food was in the oven, pots were boiling, and Souly was making a mess. Suddenly, Vivian took off her apron and vanished. An hour later, she returned, smiling and giggling. She shared that she had visited with my daughter, Andrianna, and had a great time. She then provided some anecdotes. I have seen this many times over the years and value the impact it has made on my family. I recently asked Sharif about the term *visiting*—how he uses it (he uses it often), and what it means, only to get a slightly embarrassed smile, a big hug, and the simple response, "It's just who we are."

Souly captured just that in this manuscript. He shared, in such a way that the reader can understand, the personal stories and values that form the basis of the series of visits he writes about, involving the people he loves most in the world. He asked me to edit and reorganize this manuscript, which I, of course, have not. The sense and power would be lost.

If you have the opportunity, spend some time with Souly and his family. You will be touched by their compassion, generosity, and willingness to share. Be prepared for genuine wit and an immediate sense of warmth.

Enjoy the story, and I am sure that when you are done, you will have an overwhelming urge to visit with someone you love.

Bob Katsiouleris
Singapore

In this marvelous autobiography, my friend Souly paints a beautiful and compelling picture of embracing the American dream. Hard work, fierce determination, sincere faith, laughter, love, and devotion for his family are mileposts in his journey from the land of the pyramids to the streets of an eastern Washington town. The steps along the way were not always easy. The road wound through twists and turns as it took Souly and his family from the land of his birth to his adopted community and country. Along the way, however, they found joy, satisfaction, resilience, and abundant hope.

When did we, as a nation, come to accept the shift from personal responsibility to blaming and excuse-making? When did we accept that giving up and asking for handouts would help build strong character, engaged citizens, and a healthy nation? When did we accept the shift from melting pot and integration to separation and isolation? When did we stop expecting that "your tired, your poor, your huddled masses yearning to breathe free. The wretched refuse of your teeming shore" would find hope and opportunity and weave themselves into the fabric of a growing and proud America? When did we abandon the vision of "out of many, one?" When did we leave behind the belief that we could honor our heritage while pledging our allegiance to a future we would forge together?

A country born for greatness, humbled by its mistakes, refusing to wield power for tyranny, committed to freedom, the home of endless opportunity—that is the nation Souly and his family embraced.

This story is full of reality and grit. There is no denying the hardship or rejection one encounters on the way to success. There will always be individuals who put up roadblocks, champion bigotry,

How to Become a Failure

and drape their own stupidity in the American flag. "Life, liberty, and the pursuit of happiness" are not for the faint of heart. Freedom provides opportunity for the industrious, not ease for the lazy or timid. Souly's journey does not lead him to the top of a Fortune 500 company, but it does lead him to a life of joy, a life full of wise financial insights, a life surrounded by a loving family—a life well lived. This story inspires, challenges, and offers a vision of what can happen when the rich culture of one's birth blends with the best of American values. Souly's story is our story. Souly's story, and that of his wonderful family, is a true American story.

Curt McFarland, friend and pastor
Moses Lake, Washington

Chapter One

A Title For This Book

In the search for a title for this book, I considered a vast array of options, such as *How to be Successful*, *The Road to Success*, and *Elements for Success*. We often hear of successful businessmen, entrepreneurs, and self-made people. We hear about their willpower, motivation, and self-determination. We tend to focus on success stories and enjoy gleaning nuggets of wisdom from them. People who succeed like to claim their victories and share their accomplishments. On the other hand, nobody likes to admit to failure, nor do they appreciate being blamed for it. People tend to forget or even hide anything that connects them with failure. There are numerous tales of failure that go unnoticed. We rarely wish to learn about how to become a failure.

So why did I choose this title for my book? I did not, by any means, want to discourage people from reading my story. My goal certainly was not to publish the worst-selling book. I simply tried to reflect on some of the experiences I encountered through my life. These were sometimes marked by initial failure, but many led to eventual success. How often do we hear expressions of defeat or pessimism within our circle of friends, relatives, co-workers, and acquaintances? Sometimes we find ourselves helpless or incapable of providing any advice. Other times, we get the impression that we are dealing with people who are determined to fail. How many times have you heard someone denounce themselves by saying, "I can't make it," "I'll never be able to win or succeed," "I tried, but I couldn't," "I'm afraid to try," "I know I'll fail," "I'm not lucky enough," "My parents always told me I was a total failure," "My mom told me I'd never make it in life," or "I wish I had parents who encouraged me…they always put me down, no matter how hard I tried."

Once these folks go out on their own and experience a failure, they devour the opportunity to prove their point and blame their parents for the way they were raised. They say things like, "I can't decide on a career," "I don't like this type of work," "I don't get along with my boss," or "I am overqualified for this particular job."

How to Become a Failure

Once they find what everybody else thinks is the perfect job, they might say, "I'd like to find a more challenging job," "I'd like to relocate," or "You never get ahead working for somebody else." If they happen to be self-employed, they might think, "I can live off of my parents; they're well off and have enough income to buy everything I need," "I expect a lot of inheritance money," or "Why should I work? Lots of people don't have to work for a living."

Should money become scarce, they may resort to such statements as, "I would like to get into gambling or possibly win the lottery."

All these statements reflect that they are constantly trying to fail. They want to prove to themselves and to their parents, perhaps subconsciously, that they won't succeed because their parents predicted their failures.

The object of this book is not to write my autobiography or list my achievements. It is written to show you that an average person with limited resources and great determination can decide his fate, achieve his goals, and reach his destination. In light of this, a more accurate title for this book might be *How to Avoid Becoming a Failure*.

I hope my experience as an immigrant, a parent, and a worker will help you or someone you know make positive changes to achieve your life goals.

Remember that for every hurdle you want to overcome, you need willpower. For every difficult decision you want to carry out, you need inner strength that will push you to confront new challenges and keep you going. The key words are power and control. You might have power within you, but you need the tools to unleash that power.

Be positive, regardless of what other people think. Don't confuse willpower with self-denial. Willpower is most dynamic when applied to positive, uplifting purposes. When you meet challenges in life, visualize yourself happily and busily engaged in achieving your goals.

Make up your mind. Determine your goals and targets. Believe in yourself and in your cause. The drive to feel better about yourself provides you with the willpower to overcome most difficulties. Sharpen your will and maintain routine exercises that can further strengthen it so that you can confront more difficult challenges.

Finally, expect trouble. Be realistic. Be patient. It will definitely pay off. It worked for me, and it will work for you. Work for a reward of success; foster an inner voice of confidence. You may face more difficult tasks, but with perseverance, you can conquer. Good luck, and God bless you.

Chapter Two

ARRIVAL OF AN IMMIGRANT

I was born in Egypt in 1937. I was educated in American mission schools. I earned a bachelor of science in chemistry in 1957 and a special diploma, equivalent to a master's degree, in psychology in 1962. I taught chemistry and physics for eleven years while in Egypt. In 1968, I decided to join the many immigrants who come to the United States of America each year for a variety of reasons. Some of them come to seek further advancements in their education, careers, or experience. Some, on the other hand, come to make money and become rich, with the goal of eventually returning to their homelands. Few come with the idea that money grows on trees and want to take advantage of the system until they become American citizens and have more financial assistance.

I immigrated to the United States in July of 1968. I enrolled at the University of Washington for graduate studies. I soon learned that I needed either a scholarship or a miracle to make this happen. All I had been allowed to carry out of the country during President Nasser's regime was pocket money, precisely $223. This left me with one choice: work. I was anxious to work—any job would be satisfactory. I wanted to achieve my goal of earning my own way in life while contributing to my new homeland. I was determined to make it and make it big. After all, I had come to the land of opportunity. I knew it would be difficult to find my first job. Nonetheless, I knew that opportunities were available for those who were willing to seek them out and to make sacrifices.

I had been in America for less than thirty days when I accepted a clean-up job at a potato plant. Before I earned my first paycheck, I landed on my back while steam-hosing a greasy floor at the plant. I arrived at the hospital by ambulance and then went to the chiropractor for treatment.

As I arrived home that day, the phone was ringing. "What are you doing cleaning floors when you have a master's degree?" a gentleman inquired. He was the head of the research department at a local sugar factory. I suspect he received my contact information and qualifications from the employment office.

I replied, "Sir, I needed a job—any kind of job—in order to help me achieve my goals and further my education. It is very hard for an immigrant to get his first job in the United States, and my employer pays me well, a dollar sixty-three per hour."

A long silence followed. He sounded like he was helpless and could not match this kind of offer. Then he added, "I have been trying to get hold of you all day. We have an opening at the sugar plant for a lab technician. I want you to come see me first thing Monday morning." This signaled the end of the discussion on his part and the beginning of a day of dreaming for me.

Many questions filled my mind. How did he find out about me? Why me? What could I do to impress him? How much would this pay?

And I began to think of the answers to my many questions. He'd probably learned about me from my application at the employment office. But why me? I answered with a high degree of certainty. I was sure it was because I had come to the United States with a positive attitude. I came to work, not to be a burden on society. I came to explore a new adventure with the determination to succeed. I came to live a better life with clear objectives and well-defined goals. I came with pride and integrity, seeking job opportunities. I was not willing to join the welfare recipients and waste time standing in line when I was physically capable of earning a living.

Before going to bed on Sunday night, my mind raced with thoughts of a potential job offer and what could be made of this opportunity. I inventoried my talents in order to prepare myself for a successful interview. I didn't sleep that night. It was as though I was about to catch a fish and was afraid to let go for fear of losing my reward.

When Monday came, I dressed up in a formal suit and tie. I arrived at my interview with great confidence and hope. The interview went well. I was offered the job, which paid almost twice what I made at the potato plant. Since the job title was 'lab technician,' it was more closely related to my background as a chemist. It also opened doors for future advancement. As a matter of fact, the job transformed into the position of research chemist shortly thereafter. Accepting such a position was a reminder that I had indeed arrived in the land of equal opportunity, regardless of race, color, age, or origin.

How to Become a Failure

As I shared my story with other people, I heard several comments, none of which gave me any credit or praise. I often heard: "Aren't you glad that this accident led you to the job interview for a better position?" and "Don't you feel fortunate that you were in the right place at the right time?" They all seemed to agree that I had gotten my job by chance.

I give thanks to God, who arranged the events that led to my first job. Nevertheless, I deserve some credit. I did not wait for the job to come my way. The progress and achievements that I made in a relatively short time were not by chance; they were made by choice. I chose to immigrate so I could have a better life. I chose to work rather than stand in line, waiting to collect money. I worked diligently in order to advance and further my career. If I had chosen to simply collect money, I probably would have enjoyed the easy life and become lazy. Not to mention, I would have sent the wrong message to my future children and to other immigrants.

About this time, a friend from Egypt contacted me suggesting that I make a trip back to meet a young woman whose family was acquainted with his. I welcomed the opportunity and made travel arrangements for August of 1970. I was anxious to become acquainted with Vivian and her family. I fell in love the minute I saw her. Before we knew it, we were engaged to be married.

I wanted to rush the wedding arrangements, seeing that it was going to be difficult to procure more vacation time for a return visit that year. The added costs of another seven thousand mile journey was yet another factor in not wanting to make an additional trip. However, as could be predicted, my future mother- in- law insisted that we delay the wedding for another year so we could get to know each other better. I should point out that it is common in the Middle Eastern culture for the engagement period to last at least six months to ensure that both spouses are comfortable spending the remainder of their lives together.

Therefore, I came back to the United States. After a long year of waiting, I returned to Egypt in August of 1971 to marry my beautiful wife. I had to make two trips and ended up with only one wife, but she was worth it. After the honeymoon, we made our first home in a humble apartment in Moses Lake, Washington.

Chapter Three

MY CAREER

I was satisfied and content with the lab technician job, especially since it was a step up from my previous occupation, the clean-up job. Although I felt I was overqualified for the position, I continued with a positive work ethic. I continued to write down all my observations, document my findings, and illustrate my work with microscopic pictures and photographs. I did everything I could to present a positive image of myself and to excel in what I did. I was driven by a sense of achievement and the rewarding feeling of what people called good luck.

The hard work, willpower, and determination paid off. I was soon presented with a better opportunity within the same company—the position of research chemist. This time, however, I felt underqualified for the position, especially with the rapid advancements in science and technology. The situation left me with only one choice: to confront the new challenge set before me. This enhanced my willpower and determination to meet the requirements of the new position.

Once the new goals were defined, I needed to add stepping stones to overcome the obstacles and assist me in reaching my new heights. I revisited my weaknesses and worked hard to improve in these areas. Some of the obstacles I had to overcome were language barriers, my lack of understanding of American slang, the speed of my reading, my writing abilities (including punctuation and grammar), terminology, and instrumentation. I had to work an additional four to six hours every day just to overcome some of these obstacles. That was easy for me to accept because this was always part of what I'd planned to implement in order to stay in the race. I was well prepared to do this even before I came to the United States.

In a study done at that time, Stanford University MBA graduates were surveyed on what factors produced success. Surprisingly, grades were not among those factors. Instead, the most successful individuals were those who were comfortable and confident speaking with anybody. Because of this, I learned about football, baseball, fishing, and hunting

How to Become a Failure

so I could take part in the everyday discussions that took place outside of working hours. For the first time, I learned that you play football with your hands, not your feet, as is customary in other parts of the world. I learned to set up dates (with girls) rather than eat dates (the fruit). I learned about entertainment, TV shows, and popular music. I learned about the Supremes, the Bee Gees, and the Osmond Brothers. I learned to eat hamburgers, hot dogs, and apple pie. I learned to accept ketchup with almost every meal. I learned new vocabulary and understood what it meant to be cool, awesome, and groovy. In short, I learned all I could about American culture. I made it a point to never isolate myself during social times such as coffee breaks or lunch hours.

But I knew that an overwhelming task still lay ahead of me. For the first time, I found myself falling behind. I needed more than hard work and self-motivation. I needed a stronger driving force. I constantly sought inspiration by connecting the optimism I found in small events with subsequent grand accomplishments.

All my efforts, abilities, creativity, and willpower were unleashed, providing me with the driving force I was looking for. Subsequently, I acted as though I were trying to prove a point. In my imagination, I often fast-forwarded to a day where I would tell my life story and it would sound so good that people would hardly dare believe it.

I learned that we all possess unlimited power—the power of the confidence within us. Once we unleash it, we can create real differences in our lives and can achieve what we previously thought to be impossible. We need inner strength to push us to confront challenges and persevere.

When I reached the peak of my professional career, I felt like everything was going my way until I learned of the foreclosure of the sugar plant. I lost my job in March of 1979. I was confronted with high mortgage payments on a lakefront house we had just finished building. I had just ordered a dining room set for my wife, as well as an outdoor swing set for my son's birthday. We had four children and were facing the unknown; we had to watch every penny. It is a helpless and empty feeling when you cannot provide for your children. This is especially difficult when they are too young to understand the reason for the cutbacks. Once again, I presented myself with a new challenge. Deciding to spare my wife and four-year-old son from feeling the pinch of unemployment, I went ahead with the purchase of both the dining room set and the swing set. With the anticipated shortage of money, I took a risk and made monthly payments for these purchases. I also made sure that my other children's desires were not compromised. From that point on, I promised myself that I would do my best to adequately provide for my family and be better prepared for future setbacks.

This experience enhanced my preparation for the unknown. It is a known fact that success can only promote success; however, I also believe that failure can lead to success. I decided to take this event as a detour rather than a dead end. Not only did it mark the turning point of my career, but it also helped me in the building of my financial independence and stability.

When I immigrated to the United States, I knew it would not be easy all the time. When I lost my job, I wanted more than ever before to stay in the race. I was determined to continue my journey and stay on the road to success.

When Easter came, money was scarce. My wife filled four Easter baskets with inexpensive candy. We wanted our children to experience no less than they had in previous years. We were determined to provide for our children, not only with candy and toys, but with education, self-esteem, and pride.

My lovely wife, who has a degree in accounting, did not waste any time. She got a job as a bookkeeper. Her earnings barely paid the mortgage. We continued to live on a strict budget. We raised a small garden, and I fished in order to lower our grocery bills. We cut corners wherever we could, and yes, I learned how to change diapers while my wife was at work.

Because I had lost my job at the sugar plant due to foreign competition, I qualified for financial compensation, equivalent to 70 percent of my wages, according to the Trade Readjustment Act (TRA) program initiated by President Gerald Ford. This program provided security and relief and was offered for up to two years. I knew this was only a temporary fix and a dead-end situation. I struggled with whether or not to accept this help. My main fear was that I might start to enjoy the easy life. I did not travel seven thousand miles to the United States to collect handouts. I was concerned how this period of time might look on my résumé. I was troubled that my children might get the wrong message and learn to take the easy road. I wanted to provide for them while teaching them lessons in integrity, willpower, determination, and perseverance.

How to Become a Failure

Unfortunately, there was no chance of finding a job in the height of unemployment at that time. We could not possibly sell our house in the terrible market following the shutdown. After considerable thought, I decided against taking advantage of the TRA benefits. I felt it was best for me to become an investor or business owner. I cashed in all my company savings and retirement funds and purchased a small restaurant. I experienced a sleepless night after signing the contract. I realized I might have rushed into the decision. I consoled myself with the thought that I could back out, if it wasn't too late. How would a chemist like me know the difference between cooking an over-easy egg and a medium one? How would I prevent hash browns from sticking to the grill? I was concerned about how I would maintain a smile for the customers if food was burning or I was under pressure. These are the thoughts and questions that raced through my mind on that sleepless night. At this point, I did not feel I had many options. I could not find a job. I could not sell the house. I had a family to support and had to generate some wages. After all, it was the right time to buy—the seller was motivated, and the property could potentially be worth much more when the time came to sell.

It didn't take long to realize that there was not enough money to be made in the restaurant business, especially when everybody was trying to move out of town because of the high unemployment rate. We decided to put our dream house on the market with the intent to sell or lease it. In the meantime, I continued to look for a job. My goal was to find a job that I could commute to if the house did not sell. Meanwhile, we had to hire a cook for the restaurant, and my brother agreed to manage the business. We needed to withdraw the balance of our retirement money. Thank God this mess only lasted three weeks.

A visiting friend told me that he had been awarded best salesperson of the year because of his successful sale of hydrogen peroxide. He added that his success was a result of my feasibility studies in the application of this chemical reagent in the sugar beet industry.

Upon noticing the for-sale sign in our yard, he commented, "You have a lovely, well-built house." "Why do you want to sell it?" he asked. I quickly answered, "I just heard that most accidents happen within ten miles of your residence." He interrupted with a smile on his face, "What do you mean?"

"I was joking. The truth of the matter is that things were not going my way." I told him about the small restaurant we had purchased and the struggle we had in providing for the family. Then I added, "It is almost impossible to get rich running a small restaurant. My wife and sister-in-law both work until midnight preparing Middle Eastern food each night. My brother, who is still working as an operating manager during the day, cooks while I wait on people. We are all working hard, trying to make payments on the house and put food on the table. I feel I owe it to my children."

As soon as my friend returned to his hotel room, he called me. "Have you applied for the quality control chemist job advertised in your local newspaper?"

"I can't move before we sell the house," I answered.

"You don't have to move," he replied. "It's only forty miles away from where you live."

I was eager to learn more about the job—the specifics, the operation, and most importantly, the contact person and his phone number. First thing the next day, I arranged a job interview. I used all the information I learned from my salesman friend to my advantage. I left a positive impression. I accepted the job offer after they accepted my terms. I did not feel that, under any circumstances, I should accept lower wages than I had previously made.

We had signed the contract to buy the restaurant on July 1, 1979; I started my new position as quality control chemist on July twenty-third.

I accepted this job, but I felt I had betrayed my brother, who was still working hard at the restaurant in addition to his other job. It was too big of a burden for one person. Although I hired more help when I left, I continued to go in one hour early to open the restaurant and get things ready for my brother. Then I would begin my nearly one-hour commute to my new job. After nine hours of work, I drove back to the restaurant, cleaned up, counted the money in the register, bought food and supplies, and got things ready for the next day.

Because of the favorable buyer's market and low to no down payment requirements, we were able to take advantage of this and buy more investment property. We conditioned our offers to the real estate office that the properties would be leased for at least one year prior to our purchase. I worked every single Saturday and Sunday, catching up with my duties around our house and around some rentals that we owned at the time. I would put in fourteen hours per day when needed. I learned how to work hard. I viewed myself as a horse in a race. I was driven by my commitment and desire to succeed. I was motivated by my

How to Become a Failure

children and their needs, which helped me stay on the track to success. I had promised to provide for my family, and I felt quite capable of doing this rewarding task.

❖❖❖❖❖

The quality control chemist job eventually developed into a quality control and research manager position. During my professional career, I enjoyed a great sense of achievement. I was instrumental in helping my company achieve certification in ISO quality management systems. I made significant contributions to several industries and developed many innovative procedures and techniques. I gave several presentations, published many articles, and was the author of three US patents. I am still an average person with relatively average credentials.

I enjoyed every minute of my career, but there comes a point when one must decide to move on to the next step. Retirement is one of those decisions. With a great sense of accomplishment, achievement, and hard work, I decided to retire at the age of sixty-one. For one thing, I desired to spend more time watching my children progress in their endeavors. I figured that there was more to family life than adding money to my portfolio. I wanted to treat myself, and I had all sorts of plans, from traveling the globe to owning some toys I had always wanted.

During my retirement party, I was honored and praised by many who wished my family and me the best. I value and treasure every word and gift that was shared during that occasion. "Daddy's girl" presented the most wholehearted appreciation. It was deep, rewarding, sincere, and penetrating. Those words bring tears to my eyes every time I read them. I would like to share them with you.

Dad,
I could never thank you enough for the generous way you have taken care of your family. I can only hope to do half this much for my family someday. I appreciate your managing a restaurant and traveling more than eighty miles every day to provide for us. The hard work will never go unnoticed. The special, creative ways you surprised us with your presence or a token of your love will always be remembered. You wanted nothing but the best for us in academics, spouses, and most of all, morals. We had our tough times, but it all turned out all right. I am very thankful for the many years of hard work and your innovative ways

How to Become a Failure

of becoming a successful businessman. Now it is time for you to sit back and enjoy life. I hope that we can reciprocate. You completely deserve this. I love you very much. Thanks.

Your loving daughter

Chapter Four

MY FINANCES

This chapter is not intended to describe my financial and personal investments. Nor is it my intent to educate you on the ins and outs of real estate or to share the personal ventures and risks that we took, although I may use real examples to illustrate a point. The main objective behind this section is to help you realize that nothing is impossible. There is a way to make it into the real estate market, even when you do not have enough capital, when time is limited, or when you are in your retirement years. We often hear the saying , "You have to be in the right place at the right time." I learned that you can strategically put yourself in the right place, and you can ordain the right time. Furthermore, you can even create the right conditions. In other words, you can write your own formula or prescription for financial stability and success. You've got

How to Become a Failure

to work hard, be patient, take some chances, and be prepared to adjust your plans. It worked for me, and I am certain it will work for you.

I started my new life in the United States when I was thirty-one years old. I had less than $223 in my bank account.

When I bought my first used car, I dreamed of a new truck. When I lived in a two-bedroom apartment, I hoped that one day I would live in my own house and dreamed of a waterfront, multilevel, custom-built home. When I started my career as a lab technician, I dreamed of a more challenging and rewarding position. I dreamed that on the day of my children's graduations, they wouldn't have to worry about paying back loans. When I traveled on business trips, I dreamed of being able to retire early, keep healthy, and afford to travel on my own at least three times annually within the United States and abroad. I have achieved all my goals. More importantly, I feel a sense of fulfillment.

Over the past thirty years, I bought, built, sold, and leveraged. I moved seven times within one small town in order to build equity. I traded or multiplied one rental property into two, then two into four, and four into eight, etc. I leveraged as heavily as I could throughout this phase. I made sure I paid myself first. By this, I do not mean that I treated myself with gifts and bought all the toys I wanted. I mean that when we saw positive cash flow, we reinvested almost everything. Sometimes I had to borrow: one month I used my Visa card, and the next month I used my MasterCard in order to protect some investments and make payments in a timely manner. My wife opened a daycare center in order to generate more money for investments and to meet certain deadlines and payments. In all cases, we never confused cash flow with profit. At this time we chose to get by with sheets for draperies rather than custom made window coverings for our residence. On the other hand, we always provided the best for our rental properties.

We took some conservative risks but always balanced the risk-taking with discipline. We maintained a good credit rating. We kept our rental properties in the best possible condition and catered to the tenants' needs. This was a main factor in securing high rent with minimum vacancies. Nobody put it better than Clarence Werner, who built one of the largest trucking companies in the nation. He wrote about building your own business: "Once you become successful, you thrive on motivation and start competing with yourself." I learned the art of competing with myself. I also learned to avoid competing with others. I never compared my needs with other people's needs. I was convinced that people with greater goals might look down on me, and people with lesser goals might envy me. I decided what was important in my own life and what steps I needed to take in order to ensure my success and achieve my goals. Unlike high-profile people, my venture in wheeling and dealing might serve the average person. Writing my life story in order to inform others of the ways and means for success from firsthand experience could be my main objective and best achievement.

❖❖❖❖

After four years of leasing a two-bedroom apartment, my wife and I realized that at least one and one-half years of my wages had been lost to renting rather than building our own equity. The wake-up call came when the landlord restricted our visitors from using the laundry facilities. I took this personally and refused to compromise my convenience. We realized that we had unintentionally found ourselves in the right place at the right time. It was the right time to move in order to have more freedom and fewer restrictions. It was also the right time to buy our first home. We collected every penny we had for a down payment.

We could not afford new furniture, drapes, or appliances for the new home. We used our old car to get me to work and back, to do necessary shopping, and to go to the Laundromat. We slept on the floor and used bed sheets for drapes, yet we felt blessed. When we sold that house, our profit was at least ten times the amount of the down payment and our closing costs. This profit was something we could never have achieved by leasing and building someone else's equity. At this point, we decided that we would rather purchase or build our resident home instead of renting or leasing. In this way we built our equity rather than the equity of others.

After I lost my job we could not sell our newly built home. The only offer we received reflected the declining economy of our community after the plant shut down. We quickly realized it was the wrong time, and we also realized we were in the wrong place. Being in the wrong place at the wrong time would not influence our decision or lower our determination. We were not prepared to compromise the price and accept a low offer on our dream house. We decided to find someone to lease the house from us—we needed somebody else who could make payments to us until we were more capable of making our own payments. We needed someone who could handle the high mortgage payments, utilities, and maintenance in this interim period. Granted, we would have to make some sacrifices. We moved into a much smaller home. Half of our furniture didn't fit in this home. This worked to our advantage, since we were able to lease our house partly furnished. We leased our dream home to executives of Japan Airlines for four consecutive terms, a total of nineteen years. The average monthly rent was almost twice our mortgage payment. At the end of the final lease term, this house was sold at the right time for three times its cost. Since we sold the property on a real estate contract, we took the place of the bank and made much more money from the interest at that time.

In the meantime, we could not continue to deprive our kids and ourselves by struggling to live in a much smaller house. This, coupled with my strong feelings against spending money on rent, influenced my decision to move again. At the time, we owned a vacant lot across the street from the lakefront home we were leasing out. Our plan was to build a new house, live in it, and then sell it when the right time came. All we had was the lot and enough money to pay for the foundation and possibly the framing. In order to stretch our funds, I acted as the general contractor and saved 20 percent of the building cost. At one point, we needed to borrow $15,000 from the bank. It was not enough to finish the building, but provided us with a closed room in which to store our belongings and furniture instead of leasing a mini-storage. In order to finish and obtain the occupancy permit, we borrowed an additional $10,000 from a relative, to be paid after three years with all accrued interest plus principle. We moved in to this three-thousand-square-foot magnificent house and our mortgage payment on the money borrowed from the bank was less than $140. We accomplished this by using the unsold lot, some money I had in the bank, the $15,000 borrowed from the bank, and the $10,000 I borrowed with deferred interest from a relative. Building this home also took some courage and risk; especially when I decided to act as the general contractor. Although I did not have the experience, I made up for it in willpower, confidence, and determination.

With the low mortgage payment, we generated enough funds to install custom drapes, an underground sprinkler system, and to finish the landscaping. After living in the house for eighteen months, we were not sure whether it was the right time to sell or not. The only way to find out was to assign ourselves $30,000 in profit and put the home on the market. It sold within two weeks of the listing date. The down payment we received from selling the house was enough to cover renting a house until we built a new one. Still, there was extra money to pay off the bank loan and to purchase a waterfront lot which became the site of our new home. Again, since we sold the house on a real state contract, we enjoyed collecting interest for five years prior to the pay off date of the remaining balance.

While some investors feel they are forced to defer, hide, or circulate their capital gains, we enjoyed the process of making money more than the money itself. The large sum of money resulting from the sale was reinvested in building more rentals and townhouses. What a privilege it is to enjoy a self-made fortune!

"You have to be in the right place at the right time." There is an exception to this statement. It can become a defensive statement or an excuse some people use when they fail. We are capable of deciding our destinies. If you choose to be in control, you can choose the right place, and yes, you can manage to find or patiently wait for the right time. If you think that Las Vegas is the right place, you might have to wait a lifetime until the right time comes. If you count on Regis Philbin to make you a millionaire, you may have to use all your lifelines before you ultimately realize that it is not the right place.

You can never meet challenges and advance while you are waiting for things to happen.

When I decided to move to the United States, I knew I was coming to the right place. When I decided to stay in a small, growing community, I put myself in the right place. I never bought property unless I felt it was the right time to buy. I never forced a sale or put myself in a position to sell unless it was the right time to sell.

We always chose to live in a given house and enjoy the new carpet, paint, and fixtures until it sold according to our terms. At that point, we called it the right time. We were always in control of the place and time. There were sacrifices to be made, hard work to be performed, and patience to be practiced. In our case, we moved seven times within one small town in order to watch our money grow at an increasingly fast pace. We were able to get ahead and expedite our financial gains in an exceptionally short time. In other words, not only did we feel as if we were in control of being in the right place at the right time, but we created the right conditions to achieve our financial independence and stability as we won the race against the clock.

We decided that every time we moved, we would have to make at least $30,000 profit on the sale. Otherwise, we chose to stay where we were. Thirty

How to Become a Failure

thousand dollars was equivalent to twice my wages at that time, which was in the 1970's, or at least ten times our savings in one year. In other words, by moving seven times, we advanced our savings by some seventy years. We proved that time is not our worst enemy. We used these additional savings to pay off our first property, and then it became easier to pay off the rest of the rental properties.

Throughout all these moves and transactions, there were certainly sacrifices and adjustments to be made. The outcome, however, was always rewarding, and it always moved us one step closer to our financial independence. The decision to continue investing in real estate was made when I lost my job. This was a turning point in our lives.

Once you reach your goal, you must start rewarding yourself in a substantial way. When I reached the comfort zone of where I wanted to be, I made it a point not to compare myself with anyone. Everyone is different and has different circumstances, different goals, and different objectives in life. I did not want to continue climbing the uphill battle to financial independence. I also wanted my kids to witness my hard work starting to pay off.

Trust in God and believe in your kids and their abilities. If they learn the trade secrets and how to earn their way, they can complete the road to success. They can continue to construct the pyramid to the top. If you've done it, they can do it too. They will have a head start after watching you. After all, you showed them the way instead of giving them easy money. Determine what is important in your life. What steps will you take to ensure your success and achieve your goals? Choose your plateau or level of comfort and learn when to quit. Watch your kids finish what you started.

Chapter Five

A Chat With My Daughter

One summer in the 1990's, we took the family on vacation. We spent quality time away from all routine, business, school, rentals, and phone calls. Was I up for a treat!

It seemed that all of them, including my lovely wife, ganged up against me on this vacation. The kids felt more at ease to express what was on their minds. They blasted me with a series of questions from all directions and demanded straight and convincing answers. Our conversations always began mildly, but some ended up as heated discussions. I felt cornered and that they wanted to get even with me since I used to question them often. I enjoyed individual visits and chats with each of them on a regular basis. This time, however, I was dealing with their collective efforts and thoughts. Thank God I only have four kids and one wife! Three of my kids are outspoken, and one is reserved and conservative. The one who scared me the most was Tony. He can be convincing and logical. Even though he is the youngest, his siblings chose him to be their representative during my trial.

One evening, we were sitting on the beach when Sharif asked, "Dad, out of all of us, who has been the hardest to raise?"

I told him, "You were."

He replied, "It sure didn't take you any time to answer that one."

I wanted to tell him that it took me several years to establish that, but before I had a chance to answer, Sonia interrupted. "How about me?"

"You were also tough to raise, but in a different way," I said.

"How is that?" she asked.

I replied, "You always liked to argue. You enjoyed bargaining the terms of a situation in everything, and you never took no for an answer."

"Is that good or bad?" she asked.

"It is good to a point, but not when every time I tried to stop you from certain activities, you asked questions. 'How come? Why was I the only one in my class who couldn't go camping, stay out late, go to dances, or stay the night with my girlfriends?'"

How to Become a Failure

She interrupted, "Remember, Dad, when I was ten minutes late and you made a big deal of it? I felt as though you never trusted me."

I replied, "I trusted you more than you could ever think. I always did; I always will. I probably did not want to take a chance on what outside influences may have surrounded you."

My answer seemed to trigger lots of memories, and she asked if we could talk alone. Sonia and I excused ourselves, went for a long walk on the beach, and talked about many things. I reminded her that she always thought I was trying to prove a point. She always thought she was right, but I wanted to prove that I was in charge. I would remind her with my favorite answer, "I am always in charge, whether you like it or not. I will continue to take charge when it comes to parenting. I am older than you are, and I know more than you do."

"But, Dad, I was eighteen years old, and I felt I was old enough," she said.

"Sure, you were getting older, but you can never outgrow your parents," I answered.

She continued to turn over more stones and find more issues as she went on. "Dad, let's face it, you came from the Middle East where the boys get royal treatment. They always get away with doing anything they want. I know my brothers got away with a lot more than I did."

I answered, "At times it might appear that, as parents, we are not fair, but you have to remember that each child is different, and there is no special formula that works for all children. Granted, we came from a different culture, and we often struggled between your desires and our background. We decided to adopt the best of both cultures and came to the conclusion that, when in doubt, it is better to be conservative. It is better to be cautious than to be sorry. I have to admit that we were probably still learning how to parent since you were our first child. Remember that it is to your advantage to be directed by loving parents. I never felt that I gave the boys more freedom than you. In my estimation, if I had, they might have dishonored other girls, and I do not want anything for other girls that I would not want for my own daughter."

Even though she seemed to be convinced, like always, she persisted onto the next point. "Sure, Dad, but I remember hearing that when I was born, you were tense and unhappy because you wanted to start your family with a boy, which is a big thing in your culture."

"I was tense all right. The new experience of having a baby in the house left us exhausted and overwhelmed. But you're wrong about me being disappointed that you weren't a boy. On the contrary, I've always felt that girls are calmer and less violent. They can set the precedent for their younger brothers. I hoped to start my family with a girl who would be more civilized and would bring discipline to the rest of her siblings. Don't you remember that when you got married, I walked down the aisle with tears in my eyes? Don't you remember when I stood in front of four hundred people at your wedding reception and announced that I would rather they took all three of my boys and left me my daughter?"

For the first time, she did not argue. I took advantage of her silence and continued my speech. "Sometimes parents feel helpless, especially when we cannot prove our point to our own kids. I want to assure you that I never did anything for the sake of proving I was in charge. Despite what you may think, I was not on a power trip either. It was my expression of love and my way of laying a strong foundation for the continued success and wellbeing of my family. I couldn't be prouder of the way you've turned out."

I reminded her of her letter of gratitude to me for the way I raised her. I also reminded her of the five-page letter which I addressed to her on her wedding day, a letter that reflected my true feelings for her. I had brought this letter along on the vacation and began to read it to Sonia.

To my little queen in the white dress, with love, from Dad, it read:

It has been nineteen years since we were blessed with our first little child. A new learning experience of several dimensions...you grew, and our love for you continued to grow...Soon enough you will start a new page in your life and in ours. The decision to let our only daughter go is hard for us. It feels like someone is taking a part of me away. Daughter, you graduated with honors (magna cum laude)...You gave us so many reasons to be proud, our chins will remain up forever. When you start your family, remember that your children need someone who shows love to them but also someone who will set limits. Those who do not dare to discipline will end up merely punishing their children. I know that if I had to do it over again, I would spend more time with you. I want you to know that I love you, and I always have. I am confident you will make it to the top.

"Now you are very successful in your career as a wife and a mother. For the first time, I have to admit that you are in second place, all right. Kylene,

How to Become a Failure

my first grandchild, comes first. I am glad that you followed my footsteps and started your family with a beautiful girl. Now you are on your own. I trust that you will continue the road to success that we started together. One day, your children will pick it up from there and start where you ended."

Chapter Six

An Outing With The Boys

I have always enjoyed the sense of humor and live comedy shows which take place when I meet with my sons. I strongly believe that a sense of humor, laughter, social skills, and friends are important elements on the road to success. Two days after I met with Sonia, I could sense conspiracy as I saw the boys whispering and plotting. I was completely prepared to confront and answer any questions. I intended to be open, honest, and accurate. I was hoping they would learn more about me and my values. In addition, I wanted them to become more convinced of my views on raising a family. My ultimate goal was for them to adopt these principles and values so that they could apply them to their own descendants.

The four of us sat down in a shady area and before I could even open my mouth, Tony asked, "What's up? How did it go with Sonia? Who won?"

"Won what?" I asked.

Sharif interrupted. "Dad, how about me? When is it my turn?"

"I was going to start with you, but I had a feeling you didn't want to be first," I answered.

"Why is that?" he asked.

I laughed. "Remember that year when you were in the top ten of your class? I asked you why you were not the first and I will never forget your answer—that there was already another kid who got first place. It reminded me of the time when I joined the army and the sergeant asked me to stand at the end of the line."

Ramez asked, "What happened, Dad?"

"I went all the way back and returned to tell him that there was already somebody at the end of the line...I was trying to be funny." They all burst into laughter. I interrupted the chuckling and said, "Kids."

"We are not kids any more. We are grown up," Sharif stated.

I answered, "Okay, grown-up kids, you will always remain kids so that your mother can feel young. As I mentioned to Sonia, you can never outgrow your parents. But seriously, there is a lot of truth in that end-of-the-line illustration. I have never seen two people fight over who got to be at the end of the line. On the other hand, it is different when it comes to being in first place. That is something you have to earn, something you have to work hard for. You have to be willing to succeed and be determined to make it. You must use your skills and talents to achieve your goals."

I was interrupted again by Sharif. "Dad, you're getting off topic. I have always wanted to know why you were more strict with me than with my siblings. Were you still learning on your first son?"

"Why don't you guys make up your minds? Two nights ago, I heard different from Sonia. I have to agree that we all live and learn. In your case, however, you had thick skin. You couldn't take a hint. I almost gave up on you and felt that I had to be ten times tougher in your case."

"Was I that bad?" he asked.

"Listen, Son. I'll try to help you understand. Each child is different. I remember when I looked to your brothers and sister after they did something wrong, they would cry and try to make it right. With you, no matter how strict I was, you always endured and even smiled through the punishment—but you kept repeating the same mistake. I was determined, however, to do whatever it took to put you on the right track. At times I was accused of being abusive, but this does not mean I loved you less. Furthermore, I gave all the school teachers and officials the green light to do the same."

"Did you have a plan B, in case I did not improve?" he asked.

"I always monitored and observed your continuous progress and improvement. I will never forget when you turned sixteen. We sat together in the hot tub and had a chat to remember. I told you then, 'I might have been severe in the way I raised you, but now I know that you have made a 180-degree turn.' " Tony jokingly interrupted, "You mean 360-degrees."

"Now you are my son, my brother, and my friend," I continued.

"Dad, I have no doubt that you did all of this for my own good, but I have to admit, I made some of the same mistakes over and over again because I enjoyed it." He grinned, "Remember, Dad, when you would make me leave school so that I could come home to make my bed? I really enjoyed leaving school." We all laughed.

"Why do we have to make our beds every day anyway when we're just going to mess them up again at night?" Tony asked.

"In my opinion," I replied, "it is just part of self-discipline."

"But, Dad, you never made your bed. Mom always did it for you. Did you ever make the bed when Mom went overseas?" He continued to dig.

I told him that I did not have to. I chose to sleep on the bedspread and use a blanket.

"But that's cheating," he said.

"No, that's creative," I replied. "Back to you, Sharif. I deprived you of certain activities, I grounded you sometimes. I knew that it would pay off one day. I sensed that you had what it took to be successful. I always felt you were smart and creative. You were determined to the point of stubbornness. You did things over and over, even though they got you nowhere. I remember when you were a few years old and were pushing your brother on a swing. You kept pushing him, even though the swing kept bouncing back and hitting you in the face. You still kept pushing him harder and harder, over and over, regardless of how hard it bounced back. You never seemed to make the connection."

"What an airhead," Ramez chimed in.

"No, he has a brand new brain, it has never been used," Tony responded.

"I'll never forget when your mom had to work during your infant years, and I was assigned the task of feeding you. I had to use two spoons, one

How to Become a Failure

in each hand, in order to decrease the amount of time you spent screaming between bites. Look at me, Son. As persistent as I am, I never cry when I get hungry. The main point is to be patient. You do not always get everything you want right away. Your mom always wanted to provide for you and buy everything you guys wanted. I did not necessarily agree with her.

"When you went away to Minnesota for your internship with IBM, Mom wanted to provide everything so it was readily available to you and at your fingertips. She lost sleep every time it got cold, or when Easter came and you could not be with us, or whenever we ate a good, home-cooked meal. We considered buying you a used truck instead of letting you use a bike through the snow, but I voted against this. That did not mean that I loved you less. I simply wanted you to meet challenges and learn the facts of life. I never felt that I needed to demonstrate my love to you. I was sure you sensed my love and knew that my desire was to prepare you for success."

"Dad, let's face it. When I was growing up, you constantly picked on me," he stated. "I mean, you nitpicked."

"Listen, Son, I never allowed you to get away with even the smallest of things if they were at all wrong. This held true for your sister and brothers as well. If you follow this principle to the best of your ability, big mistakes can be avoided. Sometimes you got off track. I never held that against you. As a matter of fact, I took all the blame and responsibility since I felt you feared me. When you turned sixteen, do you remember me sitting next to you? I promised you a new chapter in our relationship. I told you that one day, you would realize that I had done what was best for you and that you were never undertreated."

"What if I had worsened and chosen to leave?"

"Son, you had no choice. We would not have let that happen, no matter what. We knew that our ties and our love for you would always bring you back and keep you in the family. I remember sending you the following letter while you were in Minnesota.

Dear Sharif:
We will continue to complete our mission in life, guided by what we feel is right, what is right in our eyes and in God's eyes. Our main goal and interest is your well-being and success. At times, we have had differences. But lately, I am pleased with our relationship. I am equally pleased with your progress and trend of success. We'll do anything to raise you right. I want to make it clear to you and your brothers that there

is no room for compromising our standards. You've turned out to be a sincere, mature gentleman. You are a brilliant engineer who has had several job opportunities. Keep up the good work. I couldn't be happier or more proud of you. You have a special place in my heart. You always will.

"How do you feel about tattoos, ear piercings, and living with a girlfriend?" he asked.

"It is my strong belief that hard drugs, alcoholism, getting tattoos, and boys piercing their ears are out of the norm. I feel these problems should be addressed or treated and not ignored. My stance is that there will not be any money assigned in my will for such things unless it is used to rectify or correct the situation," I replied.

"Are you serious?" one of them asked.

"Dead serious. As far as living with a girl, it would be okay if you were animals. Animals cannot control themselves. To sum up my opinion, what I do not want happening to my own girl, I do not want happening to any other girl. Case closed."

Ramez was anxious to hear what his old man had to say about him. He lifted his eyebrows with a big smile and tried to take the lead. He didn't give me time to answer one question before asking another. I had to raise my voice to ask if I could speak while he was interrupting. We all laughed. Then I remembered that I might need a dictionary, since he was known for using big words.

He started in, "How old were you when you came to the United States? How did you meet Mom? How did you do it, raising four kids? Did you have to borrow any money? Did you buy stocks or was it all real estate?"

"Son, after you read my book, you will know all the answers."

"What book?" he asked.

"The one I am going to write," I replied.

Then he asked, "How can I read it before you write it?"

"The same difference," I replied. "I cannot answer before you give me a chance to speak."

"Okay, Dad," he said.

"I want you to slow down, Son. I will never forget when you were three years old. I parked in front of a department store and went in to pick up an order. I left you with Mom in the backseat, and the car was idling. You jumped to the front seat, shifted into drive, and the car started moving. So you started driving long before you had your license."

We laughed, and I also remembered a time when he volunteered to help his mom, who was sitting downstairs. He dragged his younger brother

How to Become a Failure

all the way down the stairs to give her a helping hand.

Soon enough, he wanted to change the subject. "So what is your book about?"

"How to become a failure," I answered.

"But who wants to become a failure?"

"Nobody, but lots of people are consumed with waiting for their good luck and fortune as they fantasize about easy gains such as winning the lottery. They don't want to have to work hard to achieve their goals. Son, if I tell you now that I have saved enough money for you to inherit—"

"When?" he interrupted.

I laughed and then asked him, "Seriously, wouldn't that change your views about how to achieve your own goals without dependence on others for your sustainability?

I know a friend who came from a rich family. He immigrated to the United States, but after a few years, he failed to meet the challenges of living in a new land and returned to his home country. It is interesting to note that he was an only son. His parents gave him everything he asked for and more. He never held a job for more than three months. He always counted on his parents' wealth and his inheritance money. He had no goals, no incentive, and no motivation. He became more and more dependent on his parents, and the minute they stopped giving him money, he became rebellious. In order to seek revenge, he wanted to fail even more so he could blame his failures on his well-meaning parents. He was convinced that his parents had abandoned him or, according to him, had not raised him right."

"I tend to agree there," my son said. "They did not prepare him to confront the challenges of life."

"Exactly," I replied. "Son, you cannot just give your kids whatever they want on a silver platter and expect them to succeed. You have to teach them to swim before you throw them into the lake. You know, kids, this reminds me of how the United States helps some undeveloped countries merely by giving them foreign aid or money. You know what? Those countries just become dependent on that help, and once they stop receiving the aid, they cannot function. Some of them even become revengeful and burn the American flag.

"Suppose in my case, as an immigrant, I had accepted the easy money which the government offers to some refugees, immigrants, and unemployed citizens. I could have enjoyed it, and then you guys could have followed in my footsteps. Imagine, Son, that they had always given you a gold medal when you were on the track team, regardless of whether you won or lost. Would you have competed, or even tried, especially if you were tired?"

"Probably not," he said.

"Right. There has to be an incentive or a reward to motivate our actions. There is always great satisfaction when you have a sense of achievement. This is particularly true as you get closer to achieving your goals. Have you ever noticed when climbing the stairs that you tend to gallop on the last three or four steps before you reach the door? Do you know why? It's because when you are close to achieving your goal, you have extra determination to reach it."

They all seemed convinced.

Ramez broke the silence. "Dad, why did you tell all your kids, except for me, that whatever education or career they chose was the right choice?"

"You know, Son, I never liked to interfere in education or career decisions for any of you. I am totally against giving a young person tough choices to make. I never wanted any of you to become doctors or attorneys if you didn't want to or didn't have what it took. But in your case, I noticed that, unlike your brothers and sister, you were undecided. I was afraid that with your hesitation and confusion, you might enjoy the comfort zone and not want to do anything. I wanted you to stay in the race. I knew you had talents that you were unaware of. I sensed your involvement and attachment to sports and statistics. You have an aptitude for math, numbers, and calculations. You were always well groomed, neat, and accurate. I visualized you as a successful accountant, auditor, or partner, but I never shared this with you. I never wanted to influence your decision. I did not want you to be what I wanted you to be. I wanted you to be all that you could be. Therefore, the only suggestion I had for you was to follow your interests and desires. Parents have insight into their children's gifts, hidden talents, interests, and strong points. Once again, your old man was right. You are doing great. You are only twenty-six years old, and you are a successful accountant with a CPA license. You purchased your house and you are a partner in some investment property. More importantly, you manage your money well. You have always been fair and accurate, with one exception."

I could not help but share this funny experience with his brothers. "One summer, Ramez wanted to invest the money he had saved from his earnings. I advised him to buy some investment property and watch his money grow. This happened after he finished community college, but before he went to a university. Since he did not have enough money, we decided to go in with him in a fifty-fifty partnership.

How to Become a Failure

He was still three thousand dollars short for his half of the down payment. He decided to sell me his car, since he would not need it. One thing he conveniently forgot was that he had yet to pay for this car. His actions reminded me of a friend who returned a can of pop and ordered a latte instead. When he was leaving, the waitress reminded him to pay. He challenged her and told her, 'I gave you the pop instead.' She told him, 'But you never paid for the pop.' He replied, 'Why should I pay for the pop? I never drank the pop.'"

"What a dork!" Tony said, laughing.

"Dad, I know I did not pay for the car, but you bought a car for every one of us when we turned sixteen," Ramez said.

"I never bought a car for anybody. I only paid the first one-thousand-dollars towards the purchase of the car. Each of you were then expected to make payments to me on the balance owed. I wanted to examine the level of responsibility in each of you. I wanted to raise you to be accountable, to manage your money, and to meet deadlines and obligations at an early age. Throughout your first year of driving, I helped you all to pay the license fees and insurance. However, I did have consequences in place if you could not meet these obligations. I am flattered that you all met the challenge. None of you lost the car of your choice. You always managed to make your payments on time to me from your summer or part-time jobs."

My son did not want to give up and asked, "Didn't you teach us how to creatively make money? Don't you think it was a smart move to try to sell you the car?"

"If you were smart, I must be dumb," I replied.

Sharif interrupted and told him, "Dad's not dumb. He's just cheap."

Then I continued, "Also, you all have established credit. I always put you as cosigners on my credit cards. You all used this wisely, except for one. When the system was abused, I had no choice but to close the account."

"You were cruel—you didn't cut us any slack," Ramez said.

Then, Ramez remembered a time when he was fourteen years old and went bowling with some friends who offered him a smoke. He gave in to the pressure. Feeling guilty, he confessed to his mother. Although my wife told me, she advised him to approach me personally. It wasn't until I took him aside three days later, knowing he was holding back, and assured him that I would be easy on him, that he finally had the courage to confess. I had promised to be considerate and kind to him if he confessed. After he got himself together and told me, I grounded him from all activities for a whole month. I readily knew what was going through his mind and told him, "If you hadn't told me the truth, it would've been a whole year."

"Did you feel guilty?" Tony asked.

"Guilty about what? On the contrary, I was pleased, and I'm convinced that none of you have ever smoked since. It seems that you all got the hint. I always believed in strict discipline. I knew that strict rules, when enforced with care and love, would produce kids who are second to none.

"You did well, Dad," Tony said, shifting anxiously as he prepared to enter the discussion himself. I was preparing myself to deal with his challenges, logic, and sharp tongue.

"Why didn't you buy me a house? Aren't we all equal?" he asked.

"Yes, you are all equal; I hate you all the same. Although you have blond hair and green eyes, just like the milkman, I have always treated you like my own son."

I looked at the accountant and told him, "Your brother comes in handy during income tax season. I need to use him as an exemption, especially this year since I have made some capital gains from stocks and got a raise."

"Wait a minute. How on earth did you, being retired and sitting on your butt, get a raise?" he rushed to ask.

"I sold a lakefront lot that we owned free and clear on a real estate contract. In addition to that, the slight cost-of-living increase from social security was advantageous. I also intend to use some dividends that I did not use in previous years."

"Wow!" he exclaimed. "So you can afford to buy me a 4x4 Toyota king cab! Or would you rather save money and give me your Lincoln Navigator?"

"Why should I give or buy you a vehicle? I worked hard to get my own. I would like you to do the same."

He jumped in. "In your day, Dad, employees used to work; but nowadays, sixty-five percent of our generation does not work —and that does not include those who have jobs. Besides, why should I work if my dad has the money?"

We all burst out laughing, and I answered, "Here we go again. How many times do you want me to repeat myself?"

Sharif took this opportunity to remind me that I repeat my jokes often. I answered, "I do not normally repeat my jokes. I only do so with you. I have to repeat them at least three times before you understand them."

How to Become a Failure

"Ha ha," he said.

We continued to laugh like we never had before. I added, "Speaking of the sixty-five percent who do not work, not including those who hold jobs, I am reminded of my first day at work at my second job here in America. I asked one of my coworkers, 'How many people work in the plant?' 'On a good day, about half of them!'" he replied.

Laughing uncontrollably, Tony said, "So you still did not answer my question, Father. What have you been doing lately besides traveling, wining, and dining? Do you have anything else to do?"

"You know, since I retired, I have worked twice as hard. Maybe I should go back to work so I can get some rest. I tell you, I have enough to do. I find it healthy to do all the manual and dirty work around here including landscaping, painting, and odd jobs. I alternate those tasks with paperwork, reading, e-mail and other correspondence, conducting business, banking, and shopping. I rest on Sunday, go to church, take it easy, and watch football.

"Every year, as you know, we take one trip overseas and at least two or three trips within the United States and Canada. These trips give me something to look forward to. Also, all my work is done in a leisurely fashion while listening to music. We often sit out on the sundeck, watching the ducks swimming and the fish jumping in the lake."

"What a tough life. Do you need any assistance?" he teased. Then he seriously added, "I have a question to ask you. Since I have only one year left before graduation, I was thinking about whether I should study only digital electronics or go for both analog and digital which will take me more than one year. What do you think?"

"I am not sure," I replied. "It may be better to graduate first and then earn an MBA degree. You can always advance and further your career and education while you are working. I do not want you to misunderstand me. We, especially your mom, would be thrilled to see you become a professional student. That way we can continue to brag that we are young because we still have a kid in school. Besides, you always earned your way through college, worked hard during the summer, and earned enough money and scholarships to pay for all the tuition and books."

"Why do you give him money every time he gets a scholarship?" Sharif asked.

"This is what I was referring to when I said that good work needs to be rewarded, and if you or Sonia had explored the possibilities, you could have earned yourself twenty-five percent of the scholarship value," I replied.

He continued to argue. "But, Dad, you never believed in easy money."

I told him, "What do you mean? How can you call that easy money? Nobody gets a scholarship unless he works hard to earn it and works hard to get it. You have to apply for it."

He reluctantly agreed.

Then, in an attempt to rub it in, I told Tony, "By the way, I invested the money you got when you sold your Nissan pickup as well as the accumulated twenty-five percent from all your scholarships, so I owe you at least eighteen thousand dollars. When do you think you will need it to buy yourself a new vehicle?"

He replied, "I thought we agreed I'd take your Navigator."

I asked, "When do you want it?"

"After it is all paid for," he answered.

"It is all paid off."

Ramez commented, "There goes our inheritance money."

I answered, "It appears as though you guys have not gotten the hint. Your mom and I decided to spend it all, especially since we cannot take it with us or drag a U-Haul truck when we go. I think Mom and I worked hard, and we deserve to be rewarded. Now it is time for you to pay us back."

Before I finished speaking, Sharif handed me an envelope with tickets for airfare and all-inclusive resort accommodations which were prepaid for my wife and I to spend ten days in Palm Springs. The kids found this to be an opportune time to present us with this pleasant surprise which they had been planning for us. Their expression of appreciation brought tears to my eyes.

"Kids, when I said it is time for you to pay us back, I never thought of this in terms of money or material things. I never want to depend on receiving money from my own kids. I meant that it was your turn to answer our questions as we attempt to keep up with the new technology. For instance, what is the best tablet to purchase, and how do I synchronize data to it?"

"So what made you think of writing a book?" Tony asked, trying to change the tone of the conversation.

I quickly replied, "I know I am not an author, but life is a book. I am writing this book as it happened. It might be a challenge to write novels. However, I feel there is no challenge in writing an autobiography. Some people are ashamed to share their books with others, while some do not have enough to share. I personally wanted to share the challenges of an immigrant who succeeded in raising some wonderful kids like you.

Tony, you are less than one year from graduating. You had two high paying internships in your field in two consecutive years. You already have more than one job offer as an electrical engineer. Good luck, and keep up the good work. I always enjoyed your candid remarks and logic, especially when you or one of your brothers got in trouble. I always wanted you to be an attorney, but I never shared my opinion or tried to influence your career decision. I knew you all had the power to be all that you could be. Also, you are in control to be all that you want to be."

That day was one of the most enjoyable times of my life. We covered many issues and answered many questions. I left this time of sharing with my children with definite goals. I decided to live longer in order to enjoy my kids and make up for all the time I missed while I was busy making money.

I concluded our time with, "There is one last piece of advice that I would like to give you while you are all here. It is time to think about finding your better halves." All three of them began protesting at once.

"I'm cool!"

"Why should I make myself miserable if I can make lots of girls happy?"

"Dad, I thought you said you would never marry again."

"Do you remember when you said that when you take your wife places it is twice the expense and half the pleasure?"

I could not make them stop. I then acted as if I was sorry that I had asked because I couldn't help but join them. "Remember when I surprised Mom on our thirtieth anniversary with a cruise to Mexico? When we got back, she complained that I forgot to buy her a gift for the occasion. She still wanted a souvenir, something she could put her hands on, such as a diamond ring, gold, or even an oriental rug."

"So what did you tell her, Dad?"

"I shared a joke with her. It goes like this:

Somebody asked his friend, 'What are you planning to do on your twenty-fifth anniversary?' He answered, 'I plan to take my wife to China.' His friend interrupted, 'But China is very far away, and that could be an expensive trip. How do you plan to top that on your fiftieth anniversary?' The man answered, 'Well, I might travel to China to retrieve her.'"

We laughed again and headed back to the hotel. On our way back, Ramez, who is always preoccupied with investment ideas, asked me how I was doing in stocks and what advice I had. I told him I would buy him lunch the next day so we could talk about it. "No, Dad, lunch is on me," he said.

Tony, who was listening, said, "Make sure to take Dad to a Mexican restaurant."

I asked, "Why?"

"So he can count the beans. He's our bean counter," he answered. I told him I didn't get it. No one had ever been able to count refried beans.

Chapter Seven

BUSINESS LUNCHEON WITH A PARTNER

The following day, exactly on time, Ramez knocked on our hotel room door. He came, as always, well-dressed in a suit and tie. Still, I wanted to pick on him and asked, "Where do you think you are going? Are you going jogging?"

We started walking to a nearby restaurant. I told him that since I was not allowed to bring any money with me when I immigrated, I brought all kinds of suits and silk shirts instead. Every time I wore formal attire, somebody asked me what had happened. "Did somebody die?" Soon enough, I learned that most of the people in the United States are more practical and more informal. This left all thirteen of my suits on hangers until I outgrew them or they went out of style.

"Do you remember, son, when you wanted to borrow one of my suits on a Halloween night when

How to Become a Failure

you were looking for a nerd costume? I remember telling you that you looked like a nerd regardless. I never expected that my nerd would become a successful young businessman, co-owner and partner with his dad, and partner in his public accounting firm. We started down the road together, and I taught you how to walk. Now you are on your own and running."

"Thanks, Dad. I could not have done it without your help," he said.

I told him, "No, Son—I mean, partner—parents are there to help. Some parents offer much more to their children than we did, but their kids achieve less. As a matter of fact, the more they offer, the more their children become dependent on them. You, Ramez, did not expect us or anybody else to do everything for you. I believe there are many uphill roads on the path to success. The more challenges you meet, the stronger you become. You are motivated by your own sense of achievement, and you can also learn from your own mistakes and failures.

"When I saw your interest in real estate, we entered into a partnership and invested in a home together. After this experience, we expected you to become an independent real estate investor.

As badly as we wanted you to be successful, we also wanted you to be responsible and independent.

Each and every one of you was put to the test at least twice. Once, when you were cosigners on our credit card accounts, and also when you were to make payments to us for your first vehicles. You always maintained good credit with us as well as with outside creditors. We wanted each of you to have self-control, learn the facts of life, and manage your money wisely. You can take advantage of credit cards during the interest-free grace period. It is best to avoid credit card debt by making sure to pay on the due date of each month."

Now I continued my discussion with Ramez regarding investments while claiming no expertise in stock market investments. I am not even sure there are experts who can predict the high and low points of the market with certainty. Nonetheless, I managed to stay ahead for some time when I split my holdings into technology stocks and conservative bonds. I used to alternate from one to the other, depending on the trend.

This, however, did not last for long because the market eventually crumbled. Everything became volatile and unpredictable. At times, it felt like a Monopoly game. Believe it or not, I used to sell my stocks before Mr. Greenspan spoke, and bought immediately after he spoke.

My son interrupted, "What if he did not speak?"

How to Become a Failure

"That would have been best," I told him, smiling. "Just kidding. I did respect his role in our economy. His moves and some of his pertinent decisions made a difference in our economic standing."

"Why didn't you sell when the market was at its peak?" he asked.

"I asked myself the same question, but how could I know it was at its peak? You can call it greed or poor planning, but I wouldn't call it inexperience. Nobody seemed to know, not even my financial advisor. I tried to pull out and buy a summer home. I saw everybody getting rich in a hurry and expected that this would drive the price of everything, including real estate, to the maximum. I did not act soon enough, however. I ended up, like everybody else, waiting until the market bounced back.

"As of now, I am still waiting. Fortunately, I was not tempted to borrow money or buy on margin. It could have been worse. I did not want to corner myself or be forced to sell at a low price. I was not willing to be at the mercy of a highly volatile market. In the past, I did not mind borrowing money to purchase property for investment purposes. I felt I was in control. I decided when to buy, when to build, and when to sell. I often made my offers contingent on the property being leased or on finding a tenant. There were always good deals out there. There were always motivated sellers. We had our choices and options, and we made our own decisions. There was risk involved but, as always, we calculated the level of risk based on time, availability, potential growth, and interest rates."

The financial rewards came slowly but surely. "My son, you started off as co-owner of our investment property. Now you own one property and are co-owner of a second. Do not spread yourself too thin. After you build your equity, proceed cautiously. If you are determined to make it, you will make it big."

As we were getting ready to leave, he offered to buy me dessert and talk some more. I could not resist his offer, especially since he mentioned coconut crème pie. Besides, I have always tried to make myself available to talk to my kids when their time permitted. As he poured some tea into my cup, he asked, "Do you consider yourself a shrewd businessman?"

"I am not shrewd, but I am not dumb either," I replied.

"Are you an entrepreneur then?" he asked.

"No, I am not. I don't even know how to spell that. I am just a chemist. I pay close attention to cause and effect relationships as I weigh situations in the real estate market. I follow the scientific

How to Become a Failure

approach: observe, make assumptions, conduct experiments, collect information, and draw conclusions. I watch other people, learn from their experiences and mistakes, and try to apply their findings to my own work and use them to my own advantage."

During my travels the year before, I met a businessman who claimed that he sold merchandise all over the world at an extremely low cost, and before I gave my son a chance to ask about it, I went on to tell him how he made his profit: from merely selling his catalog. This man claimed he had made over a million dollars in one year. According to him, everybody was interested in purchasing the best available imported products from any country at the lowest possible price.

"Recently, I transformed his idea into a similar situation, and it seems to be working. I introduced a product from a different state to some local retail stores. In order to be competitive, I sold it at cost. I made my profit by saving on shipping costs. There are incredible savings in purchasing merchandise in bulk quantities as opposed to the tremendous cost of individual shipments. You can also save tremendously when you avoid the rush by ordering well in advance of your needed shipment date. Once you become content with a small profit, the volume sales can add up in a hurry. I am currently dealing with a growing list of retail stores, firms, and corporations. There is always work to do, and there is always money to be made if you are willing to work and be creative."

"Dad, I always thought you were a chemist, not a distributor," he said.

"I am a retired scientist," I replied. "I am constantly thinking of new ideas. I want to keep my mind sharp and not become idle, regardless of whether I make money or not."

"Did you ever regret your decision to retire early? And why did you retire at age sixty-one, anyway?"

"Why not? Do you have anything against my retirement age? Retirement age in Egypt is sixty years old."

He interrupted, "But we are not in Egypt."

I answered, "What difference does that make? I choose to live by the positives of each country. I like the idea of rewarding myself. I decided to enjoy life with travel while I am still physically able."

I had long purposed that I would retire at the age of sixty. Throughout my career, I worked toward achieving that goal. I wanted to achieve financial independence. The closer I got, the harder I worked until my financial objectives were met.

How to Become a Failure

I could have retired at age sixty or younger. However, I chose to work longer to give myself more financial security. I wanted to be more prepared to confront any problems such as vacancies, forfeiture of real estate contracts, economic recession, or market downturn and inflation.

In the two years prior to my retirement, we made money at a much faster rate than ever before. As each month went by, we had more security for our future. We not only watched our equity grow, but our personal and 401(k) savings increased as well. We improved our social security and retirement benefits as we came closer to reaching our comfort zone.

The closer we got, the harder we worked. Making your wealth is like building a pyramid. The number of blocks required to reach a certain level or height decreases as you make your way toward the top. The extent of wealth you want to achieve depends on how broad the base is when you start your pyramid and, consequently, how high you want to go. A larger base requires more blocks, or more investment opportunities and adventures. In my case, I had reached my goal. The time was right. I substituted my wages for the capital gains that resulted from the sale of our investment property. Retiring early allowed me to stop climbing the pyramid of wealth. I had provided myself a reasonable income that I could enjoy while I was healthy and able.

I am proud of my achievements, comfortable with my decision, and, most importantly, I am happy with my new comfort zone. Each of my children is capable of finishing the construction of my pyramid where I left off, or they can start their own construction. They are all well-trained and have what it takes to continue to climb. They all saw me construct my pyramid and watched me being rewarded for my hard work. They also know that the sky is the limit.

Chapter Eight

DINNER WITH MY FAMILY

The last night of our vacation, we enjoyed a family dinner at a nice restaurant. We did not eat much, but we spent a good three hours wining, dining, chatting, and laughing like never before. There were no barriers, and I got to know my kids much better that night. They also learned a few things about their old man. It was a time of more questions and answers, remarks and jokes, laughter and tears. It was a prime opportunity to get everybody together in spite of their busy schedules which I could relate to. I understand the commitments and obligations that were required of them. I have been there.

Upon arriving at the dinner table, various selections of wine were served along with other drinks. It did not take a scientist to figure out what was going on in their minds.

"What happened to the dad who has been so strict and conservative all his life? What brought this change in his old age?" I bet it was easier for them to picture me turning water into wine than to see me serving them any type of liquor. I guessed right. They never expected that much of a change. Everyone wondered, "Are you the same dad we all know?"

Sharif said, "Do you remember how much you were against me joining the fraternity because of its reputation of excessive drinking? Do you remember when I turned twenty-one and you had concerns about my first drink? Do you remember how much you wanted to keep us from parties and from friends who occasionally drank?"

I thought Sonia would side with me when she interrupted all these questions. "You sure have changed, Dad," she said.

"I did not change," I protested. "I did not change a bit. Conditions might have changed. When you were young, I wanted to teach you what was right and what was wrong. I wanted to teach you that when parents say no, it means no. We continued to do this until you showed us that you were able to make the right decisions. Now we trust you and your judgment. When I visited your older brother at the fraternity house, I saw beer bottles lined up on each side of the stairway, all the way up to his room on the third floor."

How to Become a Failure

Sharif laughed and said, "But they were empty!"

"That's even worse," I retorted. "I am sure they do not sell them empty."

"Remember when you told me you were coming to have lunch with me and instead surprised me with a 9:00 a.m. visit?" he asked.

"Sure, it's all in how you look at it. I was early for lunch but late for breakfast. I learned from you, Son. Every time you were going out in the evening, I asked you to come home early. You always answered, 'Sure, Dad. I will come home early... in the morning.'" That settled the issue. They all laughed, and we decided we were even.

Being the persistent girl she has always been, Sonia insisted, "Seriously, Dad, you have really changed. I remember when I was young—"

Before she could finish, one of her brothers remarked, "That was a long time ago."

She did not think this was funny and continued to say, "You were concerned about every penny, every sale, every coupon. You closely monitored phone calls, the thermostat, and electricity usage. You were...well...thrifty."

Tony interrupted. "You mean cheap."

Sonia finished her speech. "Yet when it came time for my wedding, you went overboard. It was a dream wedding for any bride."

I told her, "My dad always taught me to save in the small things in order to make big things happen." I then shared a story I had heard in my early years, about a missionary who visited a wealthy member of his community in order to collect money for a charitable project. When he was ready to leave, the host followed him to the door and wanted to know if he needed anything. The missionary replied, "As a matter of fact, I came to ask you for a contribution to build an orphanage. I elected to leave without asking when I saw how careful you were and how thriftily you acted, especially when you went as far as carefully trying to use a single match to light the cigarettes of everyone who was smoking in that room." The host then reached for his wallet and gave the missionary what was equivalent to $1,000, and answered, "I save every penny I can on small items so I can contribute to and do big things. I do not believe in waste, but I do believe in supporting good deeds."

It did not seem that I made my point because one of the boys said, "Whatever."

❖ ❖ ❖ ❖

As I reached to refill my glass of wine, Sharif and Tony, who had lived in fraternities, each grabbed a whole bottle and acted as though they wouldn't need glasses. Tony said, "You chemists measure things by milliliters, but us engineers go by the bucket."

Ramez tried to confirm the theme of the evening. "Dad, you really have changed. You used to buy at least one house every year. Now you don't. Are you getting old?"

"The answer is no," I replied.

"So that means you are still buying property?" he asked.

"No. I am not getting old." I then turned to my alibi, my sweet wife. "What do you think, honey? Do you agree with the kids that I have changed?"

Without hesitation, she replied, "You have changed for the better. You have improved a lot!"

I sighed. "You too!"

She continued, as always, to support and echo what the kids said. "You were strict with all the kids."

"Dad, you were mean to us." Ramez stood up and started to impersonate me. "Nobody under my ceiling is allowed to do this." He attempted to mimic me in his substandard Arabic language and accent in a humorous manner.

Sharif interrupted our laughs. "When it got real rough, we used to call you President Nasser."

Tony stretched out his hand and shouted, "Heil Hitler!"

I paused and then replied calmly, as if to disprove their accusations of Nasser- or Hitler-like behavior. "Let me defend myself. I believe in leadership. Every ship must have a captain. However, the ship must only have one captain. As the proverb goes: A ship with two captains will sink.

"If we had a choice, we would have voted for Mom to be the captain!" said one of the boys.

"I'm sure you do," I answered. "I am not as dumb as I look. I know that you turned to your mom every time I told you something you did not want to hear. However, despite all that mothers provide, children feel safe and protected with their fathers. Read into it if you want; nothing can change the need for a dad. Fathers have a unique presence, a special strength for raising children. They bring a special gift to parenting. For your information, I was always guided by your mom's insight. We expressed our love to you in different ways. Her love for you was expressed by providing everything you needed. She worked tirelessly to show her love. She spent more time with you and was able to see the world through your eyes. Of course, in your eyes, she wins. On the other hand, I loved you no less. As I told your sister the other day, discipline is tough love.

Somebody had to set the limits. It happened to be me who undertook this task. Those who are cowards cannot be parents. Those who do not dare to discipline will end up inadvertently punishing their kids. I'll admit, it was painful for me to punish you four for some of the simple mistakes you made. I only did it for your benefit. I know that discipline was among the best gifts that I gave you. I was not worried about you hating me. I knew this might happen, but I figured it would only be for a short time. I had no fear of anyone leaving the house or rebelling. I was certain that the love, respect, and warm feelings among all of us would always keep us together, regardless of what shape, kind, or form of love and discipline your mother and I administered to you. I knew that if any of our children ever left the house, it would only be for a short time. I was certain you would return to your loving parents who would be waiting for you.

"Traditional values, rooted in the bedrock of mutual trust, truth, and unconditional love—these are still the keys to successful childrearing. Again, like I told Sonia, when you start your own families, please follow our route. If you are lucky, you will end up with wonderful kids like we did."

My wife interrupted the silence that followed with her traditional question. I felt like she was trying to gain support from the kids. "Ask your dad why we moved seven times. Isn't there an easier way to make money?" She knew the answer; we had discussed this topic many times before.

Before I had a chance to defend myself, Tony interrupted. "Dad likes the smell of new carpet."

I answered, "In addition to that, I had a late start and was at the disadvantage of having no money. I knew that the income from my job would not do the trick for us."

"So where did all the money go?" Ramez asked.

I told them, "We used it all to buy investment property."

"Ask your dad if we've paid off the house that we live in now," my wife said.

I answered, "I know it is a dream of all Americans to pay off their houses before they retire. As a matter of fact, we could have paid it off a long time ago. I chose, instead, to pay off other high-interest loans. Before I retired, I chose to clear car loans and other short-term loans in order to avoid high monthly obligations. However, clearing our mortgage payment was not a priority since it gave us a tax advantage."

My wife persisted. "Kids, we are only rich on paper. We do not have real security. It all comes from real estate contracts and rentals. Some money is tied up in the stock market. What would we do if tenants stopped making payments or some contracts were forfeited?"

"Now, Vivian, you know that in the past, when contracts were forfeited, we survived just fine. We avoided withdrawing money from our savings account and never felt that we were at a disadvantage. We have never regretted our early retirement."

She answered, "I know we are comfortable, but I would rather have liquid assets. I would sleep better that way."

Tony asked her, "Are you planning to put it under a pillow or a mattress?"

Ramez answered, "Neither. She is planning to buy more gold."

She rushed to answer with a twinkle in her eyes. "I love gold. I enjoy looking at gold. Besides, it is a good investment."

"What do you mean, a 'good investment?' " I asked. "Would you ever consider selling it if it went up in value? At least we can sell a piece of property or a real estate contract if we get in a bind."

Sharif joked, "Dad, you have to be thankful that you only have one wife." We all laughed.

"It is too bad I cannot return her and get a refund," I said.

"Can't you trade her in for two twenty-year-old blondes?" he asked.

"Oh, I am afraid not, Son," I replied. "I am not wired for 220."

Everybody laughed, and Ramez commented, "Are you sure you are a chemist and not a comedian? I bet if you had a big chin, you could pass for Jay Leno."

My wife still wanted to make her point. "Are you happy with the falling stock market, especially the technology funds?"

"There are many reasons to be happy," I answered. "First of all, I am happy because we don't have to sell; second, because I know it will go up."

"When?" she asked.

"What difference does it make? We don't need the money right away, yet we can use the dividends from this account."

"I agree, we are comfortable. But we are not rich," she said.

I replied, "Who wants to be rich? I would rather be comfortable than be rich. If my goal was to be rich, I would not have been able to retire early. It seems as if wealth is limitless. The more money we make, the more we spend and the more obsessed we become with making more. I compare it to the filling of a cup that has a hole in it: it can never be filled. The desire of having everything is like chasing after a mirage that can never be reached. On the other hand, if I can attain a level of comfort that is the direct result of reaching a realistic goal, then contentment is possible. The desire or need to fill the cup will eventually diminish. You can lose money and still be happy if you accept the fact that you don't need to have everything. You can be happy because you still have other resources. You should be happy because you are able to recover or adjust.

"When I started my career, I felt like I was going uphill. I figured that someday I would get tired and need to slow down. Once I reached my goal, I planned to walk instead of climb. I might even consider descending and enjoying the easier route. This means that I might start spending the kids' inheritance money. When we achieved our goals, we decided that instead of circulating all of the profit into business, we would treat ourselves. That's really about the only change in my views and life that I can admit to."

Tony interrupted with a smile. "Yes, Father, we tend to agree with everything you said... except that part about spending our inheritance money."

I replied with a bigger smile. "Inheritance money is not the answer. It could be hazardous to your future. I want you to depend on yourselves. I want you to make it on your own. I want you to be active, creative, self-made, and independent of others. Do not expect us or anybody else to do everything for you. We are here to help and encourage you. Our goal is to see you successful, and more importantly, accountable and independent. If you rely on inheritance money, you may turn out to be lazy. I have never believed in easy money.

It has been proven that unless you work hard for your money, you will spend it too quickly. We taught you how to make money, and now it is time to show you how to spend it. I am glad, in a way, that my parents did not deprive themselves in order to leave us inheritance money. I am planning to follow in their footsteps. I would also like to point out that the money I paid for my first house in the United States is not enough to buy you a used car now. With the rate of inflation, I do not expect that it will be sufficient to buy you a bicycle in the future.

"We decided to take advantage of the reasonable buying power before the expected future inflation hits. It is only fair that we spend the money we made. I am sure we can buy lots more with it now than you will be able to buy in the future.

"On another note, the government and several organizations always offer money. I do not want you to accept it. It is detrimental and could hinder your progress in life. It is a temporary fix that acts as a tranquilizer. It dulls your senses and kills your driving force for advancement. I hope that a time will come when foreign aid, financial assistance, and unemployment benefits will only be offered in the form of loans. Let's face it—who wants to work when they're being offered free money? I do not want my kids to miss out on joining the workforce. It feels good to be part of it.

"There is great satisfaction and fulfillment derived from accomplishing your goals. It is only through hard work that you can discover and actualize abilities that you did not know you had. Another reward of success is the inner voice of confidence. The drive to feel better about yourself gives you the willpower to overcome all difficulties and bad habits. Sharpen your mind, strengthen your will, and maintain routine exercises so that you are able to confront more consequential and difficult challenges.

When I moved to the United States, I did not come to collect money or to take advantage of the system. I came to work and found that there is more satisfaction in earning money than in receiving money. There is more challenge and pride in earning your own wealth than in inheriting it."

Chapter Nine

AM I READY TO DEPART?

As much as I enjoyed the thought of retirement, I was afraid to retire. I remember when my family moved to the big city of Cairo so that my siblings and I could attend college. My dad chose to stay behind in our hometown to complete his mission work as a pastor. One week later, my otherwise healthy, fifty-three-year-old father died of a blood clot. His last prayer with us is engraved in my memory. "I thank God that I completed my mission. I feel that my family can leave and be on their own."

Later we found his notes for the sermon that he had planned to preach that week. Ironically, the sermon was to be on the following passage, found in 2 Timothy 4:6–7: "For I am already being poured out like a drink offering, and the time for my departure is near. I have fought the good fight, I have finished the race, I have kept the faith."

How to Become a Failure

At the time of my father's death, my youngest brother was completing his last year of college. We all felt that our father did not leave us in the middle of the road but left us close to our final destination. My mom faithfully carried out the mission our father had wanted her to complete.

Before we knew it, my mother passed away in her sleep at the age of sixty-two. My parents are not the only members of my immediate family who have died. My oldest brother passed away three months after his retirement, and my second-oldest brother passed away soon after he retired and immigrated to the United States with his two children. He mentioned that he felt encouraged that his children were in good hands upon arriving in the United States. He was a single father who had lost his wife many years prior to his immigration. He passed away one hundred days after completing his mission of bringing his children to America.

My parents and my two brothers all passed away suddenly when they were perfectly healthy. They all died shortly after retirement. All four felt they had fulfilled their life mission before passing.

Unlike Americans, who feel that retirement is the beginning of a new and exciting life, many Egyptians die shortly after retirement. They feel they are no longer needed. Retirement in Egypt is viewed as the beginning of the end. When I decided to retire, I was left with another decision to make. I could choose the mind-set of calling it quits—being content with my achievements, the fact that I had completed raising my children and that they no longer needed me—or I could think the American way and start planning for the next stage of life. I chose to embrace the latter, and imagined ways that I could enjoy the upcoming period of time. I resolved to beat the odds. Unlike my parents and my two brothers, I did not feel my mission on earth was complete now that I had retired. I decided to reward myself and prepare to enjoy the remainder of my life. I would make choices that would help me to live longer and stay healthy. I rejected all negative thoughts, I chose to be optimistic, and to look forward as I planned how to enjoy the rest of my life. But all the planning could not prevent the next chapter of my life.

❖ ❖ ❖ ❖

On a Sunday afternoon in 2001, my life changed quickly. My wife and I were having lunch at home after church when I knew that something was wrong. I grabbed my chest and asked my wife to call 911. The ambulance took me to the local hospital,

How to Become a Failure

where I went through a series of tests. The physicians found I had an aortic dissection, and the matter was out of their control. I was airlifted to Spokane, Washington (over one hundred miles away from my hometown), where they performed emergency open-heart surgery that lasted nine-and-one-half hours. The prognosis of such serious surgery is not usually good. Upon receiving the news, Sonia made the cross-country journey to join my sons, who were at the hospital, anxiously awaiting the results. The doctors, however, advised her not to come into the recovery room, as that would imply to me the seriousness of the matter, since she had come all the way from Indiana, which is two thousand miles away.

When she was finally permitted to come into the room, I looked at her holding my beautiful, precious, nine-month-old granddaughter and weakly uttered, "Kylene." At the time, Kylene was my only grandchild. I believe this little girl gave me the incentive to persevere to health.

Although the surgery and immediate recovery went well, things soon took a wrong turn. After being home for one week post-surgery, I developed fluid around my heart and a large pulmonary embolism which was treated with anti-coagulation and IVC filter replacement. My family, friends, and church members once again gathered at the local hospital to pray for me as I was transferred by ambulance to Deaconess Hospital in Spokane for another two-week stay. Prayers were offered on my behalf all across the world. Through the power of prayer and the grace of God, I recovered.

I thank God every day for my wife, who was a rock through all of this, and for my children who were so faithful during this time. They got to know each one of my doctors, nurses, and friends who came to visit me while I was in the hospital. Not only did this experience strengthen my relationship with my children, it was also a bonding experience for my children as siblings. It is reassuring to see your children bonded to one another.

This experience caused me to reflect on the pain, grief, and sorrow of losing the loved ones to whom I have bidden farewell. Our lives have equal amounts of joy and heartache, light and darkness. We appreciate the taste of sweet, especially after we have tasted bitterness. Our memories contain anguish and frustration. They also contain pleasure and contentment. Those experiences provide us with a way to reach the future. The past is a bridge with the present that extends into the future. This gives our lives another dimension, adds more depth to our existence, and helps us understand the meaning of continuity.

How to Become a Failure

The unfulfilled dreams of our loved ones can give us the power to execute those dreams into achievements. Our parents, who provided love and support, would be pleased if they could witness our footsteps. Our lives are a continuation of theirs and of their legacy left to us. Their legacy gives us the strength to complete what they could not finish.

Chapter Ten

Meet My Family

I am Souly Atalla Farag. I was born in Upper Egypt in the year...... let's just say, a long time ago. It took my mom three nights and four days to deliver me. I was told that she went through hard labor and excruciating pain. All the relatives gave up on her and on my safe delivery. They made arrangements and preparations for the worst. My father, on the other hand, never gave up. He got down on his knees and pleaded with God. He fasted, yet he remained full of energy and faith that God would provide a miracle. He prayed to God and pleaded loudly and intensely, demanding a miracle. He was certain that God would not forsake him in a time of need.

Finally, the Lord answered both prayers, granting a healthy delivery for me and safety for my mother. The decision was made to name me Souly, which is not a common name. Souly is from the

Arabic word *Soual* (sue-al), which means *question* or *request*. *Soualy* (sue-al-ee) means *my question*. My father was a Protestant pastor with a strong faith. He believed in "Ask and it will be given to you; seek and you will find; knock and the door will be opened to you. For everyone who asks receives; the one who seeks finds; and to the one who knocks, the door will be opened" (Matthew 7:7–8).

Whenever my father was asked why he named me Souly, he would reply, "It means *the son of prayers*."

My father's full name was Reverend Atalla Farag. Atalla means *gift of God*, and Farag means *ease* or *relief*.

I find it difficult to forgive myself for all the pain and frustrations inflicted on my family members during my entry into this world, but I am worth it, I guess.

GOD

God is the center of our home. He is our Creator, our Refuge, and our Redeemer. Our living God is almighty, everlasting, and eternal. He is our Healer and Deliverer. He is our Mighty Rock and our Foundation. He keeps our family in place, in order, and in good standing. He has met our needs in the past, and He promises that

He will never leave us nor forsake us. He is our hope in all times, the trustee of our children and grandchildren for generations to come. He guards and watches our every move as He protects us from all evil. He comforts us in sorrow. He heals us when we are sick. He finds us when we lose our way and go astray. He protects us and saves us when we are in danger. Thanks be to God.

My Wife, Vivian

Vivian is my love and partner. She is my rock and my hero, my nurse and my angel. She also was born in Upper Egypt some time ago. I would not dare to tell you when. All I am allowed to say is that she is still young and will always remain young. She is also a survivor because of her endurance in putting up with me for many years.

For many years she was a silent partner, but not anymore. Watch out when she gets mad. She erupts and becomes bossy. Her tone of voice changes as she takes command with a deep voice. I joke with my boys and tell them that she has become the head of the household; that she is the man. We started signing our greeting cards to our children, "Dad and Dad."

One time, before I ended a phone conversation with Tony, I asked him, "Do you wish to talk to your dad?"

He replied, "Just tell her hello."

Another time, when we were coming back from a trip, I told Sharif, "We had to stop at a rest area because your mom had to go to the ladies' room."

He asked, "Why? Was the men's restroom occupied?" We constantly find ways to keep each other laughing in our family.

I love my wife dearly. She has been our safety net all these years. Every time I got angry, which was more common when our kids were growing up, she served as the mediator. She has a special and unique ability to calm me and everybody else. She distributes love, a gentle touch, and tender care to all children, including myself. She often tells me that I am just a big child.

Sacrificing her work in the field of accounting, the field in which she had received her degree, she began a daycare center in our home. This forfeiting of a professional career allowed her to tend to our children while earning a living.

I have to admit that she spoils me rotten. I cannot remember a time when I have made our bed or washed the dishes. I still need to learn how to operate the washer and dryer, among other household duties. With that being said, I have never been able to deliberately turn my wife down when she asks for help in the kitchen. One time, however, there was a basketball game I intended to watch, and yet I knew that my wife needed help in the kitchen. I cleverly thought to sprinkle some sugar on our black kitchen countertops and sprinkled black tea leaves on our light gray floor tiles. As soon as she saw that, she kicked me out of the kitchen. I have repeated this trick a few times, and it always works! However, now that she knows my trick, I have to periodically come up with different materials that still add a contrast to the dark countertops and lightly colored floor.

❖❖❖❖

I am often asked, "Did you know your wife before you came to the United States?"

The answer is no.

"Did you marry her because she was Egyptian?"

Still the answer is no.

How to Become a Failure

People often ask if I considered marrying an American before making two trips back to Egypt to marry my wife.

I reply, "When I came to the United States at the age of thirty-one, most of the American women were married. To answer your question, I do like American women. As a matter of fact, I like women from every part of the world. I am an equal-opportunity man. One distinct advantage of marrying an Egyptian was that I wanted to make sure my mother-in-law was at least seven thousand miles away. Furthermore, I deserve the best, and I got the best."

SONIA

Our first child, Sonia, was born on July 1, 1973. She was, is, and will always remain "daddy's girl." I always tell her that she is my favorite daughter. She then reminds me that she is my only daughter.

July first became a very lucky day in our family. Not only was this the birthday of our first child who greatly inspired me, but her birthday became synonymous with prosperity as well. I received a substantial seventeen percent salary raise. As coincidental as it may seem, *my first publication and my first US patent were also issued on July first of consecutive years. I convinced myself that not only would my daughter bring me luck, but also that good things would happen on July first.*

Sonia earned a college degree in mathematics and taught high school math for approximately five years. Upon the arrival of her daughter, Kylene, she chose to be a stay-at-home mom. She ran a business from home, tutoring math, while her kids were young. Today she homeschools her gorgeous, well-behaved children, Kylene and Brandon.

Kylene and Brandon are the joy of our lives. I tell Sonia, "Why do you have such great kids? I never did!" Her children have an inner power that extends our lives, making our days brighter and happier.

Sonia is happily married to her wonderful husband, Steven, who is a mechanical engineer. He is currently employed as a reliability engineer in the biodiesel and ethanol industry.

Sonia is very energetic, born to be a multitasking, hyperactive mom. She only gets tired when she sits down. Vivian and I get tired just watching her work. She performs multiple household chores while talking on the phone to us. I have, on several occasions, asked my son-in-law to find another wife to help Sonia out.

Her dedication to her family and service to others is admirable. Her immediate family had the privilege of serving in an orphanage in Egypt for nearly a year and a half. Committed to helping others, she seeks to glorify our Lord in response to His great sacrifice. May God bless her and her family.

SHARIF

Sharif is our oldest son. Raising him was a challenge. I have come to believe that his goal was to discipline me. Over the years, I received numerous tardy slips and complaint notes concerning him. I was a part-time parent and a full-time detective. I worked as a liaison between his teachers and the school principal. When he went to college and joined the Greek system, he became a typical fraternity kid. He made sure that his beer bottles were always empty.

I taught him some facts of life, but he taught me the character trait of patience. He taught me how to deal with pierced ears on males. In addition, I learned how much it costs for the plastic surgeon to correct this unacceptable behavior. This outrageous price, which he had to pay, *ensured that he would not be tempted to try it again. He kept me abreast of traffic violations. I owe him a lot. I learned, with his help, that I cannot be a coward and expect to be a parent. He taught me what tough love meant. He managed to turn me into a loving disciplinarian.*

At times, I was afraid he might rebel and leave the house. I was almost certain he would get even with his old man. Contrary to my expectations, he, as well as his brothers and sister, were simply respectful and loving to me.

Sharif has given me all the love, care, and attention I could have wanted from a son. He gave his grouchy old man much more than I could have ever expected. Through our journey, we learned not only how to cope with each other, but how to bond, blend, and connect. I found myself dealing with a growing, sincere gentleman. Granted, he sometimes got off track. I do not hold that against him. In a way, I feel responsible for his behavior. I celebrate the fact that he was able to feel our love and determination through the years.

I reminded him of his GPA during his first year in college, which was below a 2.6. When I asked him. "What is it with your GPA equivalent to a C average." He tried to be funny as he responded with, "Dad, the professor does not issue D grades." Holding back my laughter, I gave him a chance to improve or else severe consequences would be put into practice. He built his GPA up gradually and, by the time he graduated, it was 3.79.

After he earned his bachelor's degree in electrical engineering, he earned his MBA. Currently, he is a principal group program manager at Microsoft.

Sharif has a special place in my heart. We pick on each other. He calls me nitin—an Arabic work for miserly. One year, I decided to get back at him and demonstrate what nitin could really mean. I wrapped up one shoe for his birthday on December fifteenth. He was most concerned that the second shoe was lost. I assured him he would receive the match the following year. When we opened presents that Christmas, he was pleasantly surprised to find the other shoe wrapped as his Christmas gift. He was satisfied, not because he had received the other shoe, but because he had confirmed that his dad really was cheap.

As I mentioned, we enhanced our father-son relationship over the years. He became my shadow, my friend, and my consultant. Sometimes he defended me even when I was wrong. One time, he walked in while my wife was complaining about the time she returned from the hospital after giving birth to one of our children only to find me watching Monday night football. Sharif asked his mom, "What's your point?"

He plans to use me as his best man when he gets married. I asked him to take his time and enjoy his life to the fullest. I warned him that it will get tough after the first year of marriage. He asked if it will improve later. I said not necessarily, but you'll get used to it. He replied, "Dad, remember that I have no control over when I get married because, like you always tell me, marriage is like a heart attack; it can happen to anyone at any time."

As much as I hope to someday stand in as his best man, he has stood by me in times of need. He never left me unattended during my long stay in the hospital following my open-heart surgery. At that time, he was working as a strategic program manager for Intel. The company granted him as much time off as needed to tend to me. I would like to take this opportunity to publish my gratitude and sincere appreciation to the Intel management staff. By the grace of God and the understanding of Intel, my life was *enriched through having my son near me during my recovery. My gratitude to the management there will remain engraved on my heart.*

RAMEZ

Ramez is my middle son. He was my partner in business and later became a partner with an accounting firm. He worked in the bankruptcy unit for the Washington Employment Security Department for a short time while maintaining his own tax accounting business. He earned his bachelor's degree as well as a CPA certificate. We use his services to prepare our IRS returns. We always end up paying, whether we itemize or not. We can't help but call him Uncle Sam. He is happily married to Heather, a teacher and speech therapist. They are the proud parents of Hunter and Rihana.

Ramez is sharp and skilled in numbers—a human calculator, if you will. He enjoys sports of all kinds. He and his family watch and attend any basketball or football game they can. All of them, including eight-year-old Hunter, know the names of most players. Hunter himself is an athlete. Taking after his father, Hunter enjoys soccer, basketball, golf, and swimming. Like my other children, Ramez calls me cheap. I'll let you be the judge. One year, when we were celebrating his birthday, I deliberately gave him a greeting card that said "to my daughter." As soon as he opened the card, he blushed and was speechless in the shy manner characteristic of him. He thought I had started to lose it in my old age. When he had recovered, he grinned as he exclaimed, "Dad, you apparently weren't paying attention when you picked out this card."

I replied, "I had to buy it, Son. It was on sale." He still insists on calling me cheap.

Unlike his dad, he tends to buy everything he sees. He buys toys in every shape and form regardless of the price tag. He has a hard time resisting the purchase of many items such as furniture and rugs. He cannot say no to any sales representative. The minute he goes to a presentation, we know he will end up buying a condo or timeshare. He does not seem to believe in "give us today our daily bread." He stocks up on his supplies for many weeks. If he ever gets bored, he buys things off the Internet.

Once again, I'll take some blame for this. I had too much control over him and limited his spending when he was young. One time, I made sure he had no money in his possession when we went *to a department store. Later, I was paged to the manager's office. He had been caught by the department manager after attempting to shoplift a cap. I was furious and lost my temper. Before any further dialogue the police had arrived to settle the matter regarding the shoplifting.*

This event was a turning point for both of us. I am proud to tell you that he turned out to be an honest young man with high integrity. As for me, I stopped to reflect on what I could have done wrong. Unfortunately, I cannot push rewind. I hereby advise my kids and you to be moderate. We should calculate the effects of how we treat our kids and the consequences of every move or method when it comes to raising our children. We should think about how every move we make now could interfere and affect our children in the future.

Tony

Tony is our youngest son. We were hoping for a girl, but we got him. His name was unisex (with a minor spelling change).

He is the one with green eyes and blond hair. I have no complaints whatsoever as long as we can claim him for income tax return purposes. I was pleased to meet two members of his mother's side of the family who both are blue-eyed blonds. I remembered from my history class that Napoleon Bonaparte, the emperor of France, invaded Egypt from 1798 to 1801. This shed some light on the French influence in Egypt which explained the green eyes and blond hair. This brought me a little peace of mind.

Tony is a calm spirit who enjoys life to the fullest. This is primarily because he is not married and he can afford to buy all the toys he wants.

He earned his bachelor's degree in electrical engineering. He also earned his master's in computer science. Currently, he is self-employed and develops custom mobile software. He is sharp and nice looking. This confirms that he is my son.

He does not call me cheap, but instead he calls me gillis, an Arabic word for dull or boring, since I am known to repeat jokes. I had a chance to get even with him as he started his college career at the University of Washington, when he was asking others for letters of recommendation. I asked one of his high school teachers to give him the letter of recommendation, which he requested, in a sealed envelope. In the meantime, she sent another letter of recommendation, the

How to Become a Failure

authentic one, with his sister, who taught at the same school at the time.

When he arrived home, he was eager to open the letter. The letter read as follows:

> To whom it may concern:
> I have had the unfortunate experience of having Tony Farag in class for the last three years. During that time, I found him to be rude and highly obnoxious. He is a constant troublemaker and a loudmouth. I find him to be the least likely candidate to succeed in college because he is never done with his homework. He continually bribes people to write his papers and never pays them.

Tony was in disbelief as he read the letter. He became disturbed and choked up as he continued to read.

> Tony also considers himself to be a great athlete, but he cannot chew gum and walk at the same time. He feels this world owes him a living and will probably end up on welfare when his dad kicks him out for being a lazy bum. Tony has never worked a day in his life. He never sees the light of day before noon and is known to party until the wee hours of the morning. It is with this

in mind that I write this letter to not recommend Tony Farag for any scholarship, because he will undoubtedly flunk out.

Regards.

Luckily, as he was finishing, his sister arrived with the true recommendation...that made his day.

Chapter Eleven

MY FINAL THOUGHTS TO MY KIDS

One day I might go to sleep and never wake up. One day I might have to ask Mom to rush me to the emergency room or call the ambulance. Someday I will not be around to embrace you, encourage you, or comfort you.

I am not worried about being forgotten after I die. My desire and request to you is this: to not remember me as having been a monster while I raised you. I would like to be remembered as a loving father, a wise counselor, and a fair coach. Even though I am not nice looking, you can still remember me as your cheerleader. Remember when I watched all your sports activities. Please remember me as having been your sincere brother when you grew up. Remember the breakfast and lunch dates I have enjoyed with each of you.

I seldom end our phone calls with the obvious "I love you." I shouldn't need to tell you what you already know. I have always sensed our mutual love. But so you'll always know, I hereby proclaim to you and to the whole world that my love for you is eternal. It started even before you were born, and it will last until I die.

Although this book ends, the characters will never end. I thank God for you and that you are who you are. I could not ask for better kids. Thank you for a beautiful trip. I hope you learned from me as much as I learned from each one of you.

I would like to leave you with a few thoughts and with a request. In order to succeed in life, you must do the best you can, where you are, and with what you have. You must be ready to not only take opportunities, but to make them. Remember that you can be destined to succeed if you are determined to succeed. Choices, not chances, determine destiny. Do not be afraid to take a big step. Accept challenges in life. To be a winner, set your goals, commit yourself to those goals, and then pursue your goals to the best of your abilities.

Remember that many people who fail in life are those who did not realize how close they were to success when they gave up. There is always room at the top.

How to Become a Failure

I would like to add that I have decided to live, or at least try to live, the way I have always wanted- with dignity, courage, honor, and composure.

I hope I have given you my thoughts, my experience, my advice, my heart, and my all. At this point, I will be able to go in peace. I will not worry about being forgotten. I will feel that I did my share, and that could be my best achievement in my life.

On a different subject, mom and I have prepared some information that you may need. This includes a list of contacts such as our attorney, accountant, insurance agent, financial planner and mortgage holders. It also includes our investments, pension benefits, monthly obligations and debt, if there is any. Furthermore, our final wishes will be spelled out and attached to our will.

Let me close by reflecting on my everlasting love for my grandkids. I have always told Sonia and Ramez, "I love you, but I love your kids more." My sincere appreciation and love to you, my children, and to all my grandkids—not necessarily in that order.

One more request that I make of you, my sons and my daughter to whom I have committed my life: keep the sense of humor alive.

To Those Considering Immigration

A message in Arabic follows on the next page

It is common to see repeated advertisements by legal firms dealing with immigration laws and immigration asylum, immigration family petitions, and more. They offer help and counsel for areas such as immediate relatives category and family petitions through the preference system. Some attorneys advertise their expertise in asylum cases for Middle Eastern Christians. These ads are increasing in several states such as Florida, New York, and California.

The road is not as easy or as extravagant as most people think or wish. It is imperative to plan how to overcome obstacles. Plan your future and come prepared to work vigorously toward achieving your goals. Be prepared to sacrifice, work hard, and hope for the best. I wish you all the best of luck.

Souly Farag

رسالة من القلب الي اخواني المصرين والعرب

نظرا لعدم الاستقرار ولضيق فرص العمل في بلادنا العزيزة، لقد تزايد عدد الراغبين في الهجره الي استراليا، كندا والولايات المتحدة الامريكيه. ولقد لاحظت الكثير من الإعلانات لخدمة ولتسهيل فرص العمل للمهاجرين ، وعلي سبيل المثال :

- خدمات الاقامه عن طريق العمل وكيفية الحصول علي تصاريح العمل وكيفية تجديدها.

- تجديد تأشيرات الدخول واستخراج وثائق السفر.

- رفع القيود عن طلبات الإقامة وتسهيلات الهجره لسبب اللجوء الديني او للزواج من الأمريكان.

- الحصول علي كارت الاقامه والقرعه العشوائية.

- تقديم امتحانات الجنسيه الامريكيه باللغه العربيه او الإعفاء من الامتحان لأسباب صحيه.

أضف الي هذا العديد من الإعلانات عن فرص الاعمال الحره مثل شراء محلات تجاريه، محطات بنزين ، وحدات سكنيه، مطاعم ومقاهي ، محطات غسيل سيارات ، سوبر ماركت ، بالاضافه لشراء أراضي للبناء والاستثمار.

انني انصح كل من يفكر في الهجره ان يتروي ويحسب الإيجابيات والسلبيات. الطريق صعب والمشوار طويل ويحتاج الي كثير من التضحيات وخاصة في بداية الطريق. ارجو منكم عدم الإقبال علي اي موضوع قبل دراسته دراسه موضوعيه مع ضرورة استشارة محامي قبل توقيع عقود البيع مع جميع الأطراف المعنيه .

تذكروا ياخوتي الأعزاء ان الشعور بالغربة والحنين الي الوطن سيلازمكم طوال المدة وانتم بعيدون عن أهلكم واحباؤكم .

انا شخصيا يراودني الحنين والرغبه الي الرجوع لكي اخدم حيثما كان مسقط راسي وسط أهلي واصحابي .

ارجو من الله عز وجل ان يسدد خطاكم مع أطيب تمنياتي لكم جميعا بدوام التوفيق والنجاح .

Vivian and Souly

My Children

Top left: Sonia, eldest; Top right: Sharif, eldest son;
Bottom left: Tony, youngest son;
Bottom right: Ramez, middle son

Top: Sonia, my eldest, her husband Steve, and her children, Kylene and Brandon;
Bottom: My middle son, Ramez, his wife Heather, and his children, Hunter and Rihana

My Grandkids

Benediction

*To the most precious people to whom I have committed my life,
my sons and daughter.
Someday you will see me, old and illogical in my behavior.
At that time, I ask you to please give your time and patience to try to understand me.
When you see my hands shake, and they drop food on my chest,
when I cease to be able to put clothes on myself,
remember the years that passed when I taught you to do what I can't do today.
If I repeat my words, memories, and jokes, do not be angry.
I repeated many stories and actions for you just to make you happy.
If I become unattractive and smell,*

Souly Farag

*do not blame me, but remember that in your childhood, I tried my best
to make you look attractive and smell good.
Do not laugh at me if I do not understand your generation.
Be my eyes and my mind so I can catch up on what I missed.
I was the one who disciplined you,
I was the one who taught you how to face life,
so how do you teach me today what should and should not be!
Do not let my failing memory or my slow speech bore you,
My happiness now is only to be with you.
Help me to only do what I need.
I still know what I need.
Have mercy on me in my old age and weakness.
Take my hand,
for tomorrow you will look for someone to hold yours.
Oh, would youth know...
I wait on death. Be with me, not against me.
Forgive my sins,
cover my loins.
May God forgive and cover you.
I was with you when you were born,
so be with me when I die.*

How to Become a Failure

***Your smiles and laughter give me joy.
Do not deny me your friendship.
May God protect and guard you after I am
gone. Amen.
Faithfully,
Dad***

Epilogue

At the time of submission for publication, I am recovering from a second open-heart surgery performed by the same surgeon who operated on me in 2001. This time the surgery was planned and recovery has gone well. I have learned many lessons during this time of enduring and healing. I feel a transformation and renewing of my mind through my recovery. I feel empowered to discern God's will, as I have experienced a greater capacity to empathize with others and forgive. It is my intention, as I make a complete recovery, to share my thoughts and revelations in a second publication.

Made in the USA
San Bernardino, CA
29 December 2014